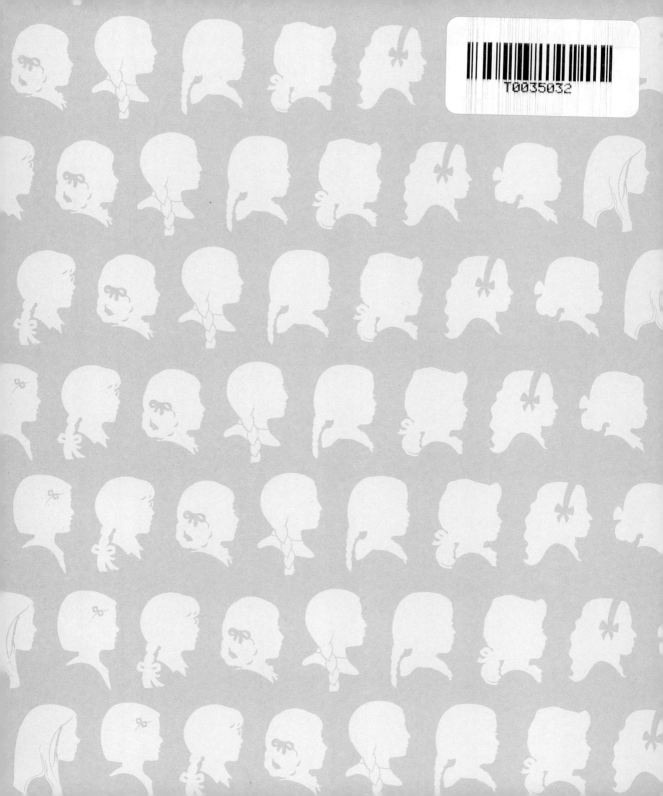

Pan-Seared Fish Tacos, page 72

Strawberry Icebox Pie, page 127

American Girl®

Sweet & Savory Treats Cookbook

DELICIOUS RECIPES INSPIRED BY YOUR FAVORITE CHARACTERS

Photography **Nicole Gerulat**

weldon**owen**

Contents

Cookies & Bars

Cakes & Pies

Introduction

For over 30 years, American Girl has celebrated girlhood with stories of family and friends, new ideas and treasured traditions, hard times and happy celebrations. Characters from as far back as 1764 have shown us that while much has changed over the centuries, gathering for a meal or sharing a sweet treat is still a cherished part of growing up.

In these pages, you'll celebrate all the girls who came before you with recipes inspired by 17 beloved and iconic American Girl characters and their unique stories, passions, and personalities. Braid the challah that Rebecca's family would have baked for Shabbat. Serve up some hummus alongside fresh veggies that Molly would have grown in her victory garden. Make the fruit leather that Blaire would have shared with visitors to her family's farm. Or celebrate Joss with some beach-inspired seashell madeleines.

Top Cooking Tips

No matter where you are in your culinary journey, these important tips are here to help you start off your next cooking project on the right foot.

Safety First!

Don't be afraid to ask for help! Adults have culinary skills to share and can help you stay safe in the kitchen Always have an adult on call to help you with hot ovens, sharp objects, and electric appliances. The hand symbol appears throughout the book to remind you that you'll need an adult to assist you with all or part of the recipe. Ask for help before continuing.

Stay organized!

Staying organized and paying attention are important cooking skills. The first step is always to read the full recipe and ingredient list. Then it's time to clear a clean work surface and lay out all your tools and ingredients. Before you start cooking or baking, measure the ingredients and prepare them as directed in the recipe.

Know your tools!

Soon you'll be cooking like a pro, but before you start, make sure an adult is there to help you choose and practice with the correct tools for the job. If you're using a knife, hold it firmly at the base and place the knife somewhere safe so it can't fall on the floor. If you're handling hot cookie sheets, have an oven mitt handy. And don't forget a timer!

Celebrating American Girl Historical Characters

In the pages ahead, you'll meet these 17 beloved characters and learn more about their unique stories—with recipes inspired by the time and places each represents.

Kaya - Kaya'aton'my
1764 ✦ Pacific Northwest

- *Frozen Yogurt Berry Bites*
- *Spiced Applesauce Muffins*
- *Nut, Seed & Fruit Granola Bars*

Addy Walker
1864 ✦ Philadelphia

- *Ice Cream Bonbons*
- *Southern Tea Cakes*
- *Cast-Iron Corn Bread*
- *Sweet Potato Pie*

Felicity Merriman
1774 ✦ Virginia

- *Sweet & Salty Peanuts*
- *Ginger Cookies*
- *Chocolate-Caramel Bundt "Election" Cake*

Rebecca Rubin
1914 ✦ New York City

- *Potato Latkes*
- *Challah*
- *Chocolate-Vanilla Sandwich Cookie*
- *New York Cherry Cheesecake*

Josefina Montoya
1824 ✦ New Mexico

- *Chile-Corn Muffins*
- *Mexican Wedding Cookies*
- *Mexican Hot Chocolate Cookies*
- *Dulce de Leche Crepe Cake*

Kit Kittredge
1934 ✦ Ohio

- *Peanut Butter–Chocolate Buckeye*
- *Sweet Potato Chips*
- *Mac-&-Cheese Cups*
- *Apple Bread Pudding*

Kirsten Larson
1854 ✦ Minnesota Territory

- *Jam Twists*
- *Swedish Meatballs with Sour Cream Sauce*
- *Pink Velvet Cupcakes with Strawberries*

Nanea Mitchell
1941 ✦ Hawaii

- *Hawaiian Chicken-Pineapple Keba with Mango Sauce*
- *Mini Coconut-Lemon Bars*
- *Vanilla Chiffon Cake with Tropical Fruit*

Molly McIntire
1944 ✪ Illinois
- Ice Cream Sandwiches
- Hummus with Victory Garden Veggie Dippers
- Red, White & Blueberry Sheet Cake

Luciana Vega
2018 ✪ Virginia
- Cosmos Doughnuts
- Moon Pies
- Fresh Peach Salsa with Star Chips
- Sugar-&-Spice Star Sandwich Cookies

Maryellen Larkin
1954 ✪ Florida
- Almond Energy Bites
- Pigs in a Blanket
- Cowboy Cookies

Blaire Wilson
2019 ✪ New York
- Homemade Fruit Leather
- "Cheesy" Kale Chips
- Mocha Chocolate Brownies
- Fresh Peach Pie

Melody Ellison
1964 ✪ Michigan
- Garden Caprese Tomatoes with Pesto
- Spiced Molasses Flower Cookies
- Pineapple Upside-Down Cake
- Strawberry Icebox Pie

Joss Kendrick
2020 ✪ California
- Pan-Seared Fish Tacos
- Sand Dollar Snickerdoodles
- Seashell Madeleines
- Day at the Beach Cupcakes

Julie Albright
1974 ✪ California
- Cheese Fondue
- Deviled Eggs
- Carrot Cake with Cream Cheese Frosting

Kira Bailey
2021 ✪ Australia
- Butterscotch, Coconut & Macadamia Nut Cookies
- Caramel Squares
- Fruit & Cream Pavlova

Courtney Moore
1986 ✪ California
- Cheese & Chive Crackers
- Savory Ranch Popcorn
- Chocolate, Vanilla & Raspberry Swirl Cake

Sweet
Snacks

Frozen Yogurt Berry Bites

Berries were a staple of the Nez Percé diet. They were eaten fresh and dried as part of the winter food supply. The huckleberry was the most popular, and Kaya would help gather them in the mountains in late July and early August. A mini muffin pan is ideal for making these frozen treats, but silicone candy molds also work well. Use your favorite berry-flavored, whole-milk yogurt, such as strawberry, blueberry, raspberry, or blackberry. You can also use vanilla yogurt if you like.

MAKES 24 BITES

1 ½ - 3 cups berry whole-milk yogurt

24 small fresh berries, such as blackberries or raspberries

 Line a 24-cup mini muffin pan with foil liners.

Spoon 1 to 2 tablespoons of the yogurt into each prepared muffin cup. Top each portion with a berry.

Place the muffin pan in the freezer until the yogurt is solid, about 1 hour.

Transfer to a serving bowl and serve.

Sweet & Salty Peanuts

In colonial Williamsburg, families welcomed guests with refreshments, like this easy snack. If you like, swap out the peanuts for roughly chopped pecans.

MAKES 8 TO 10 SERVINGS

Nonstick cooking spray

3 cups raw peanuts

½ cup sugar

Flaky or coarse sea salt

Preheat the oven to 300°F. Line a rimmed baking sheet with aluminum foil and spray the foil with nonstick cooking spray.

In a heavy saucepan over high heat, combine the peanuts, sugar, and ⅓ cup water and bring to a boil. Boil, stirring often, until all the liquid has evaporated and the mixture is pasty, 20 to 25 minutes.

Remove from the heat and pour the mixture onto the prepared baking sheet. Spread the peanuts in a single layer, breaking up any clusters, and season generously with salt.

Bake, stirring once, until deep brown, 30 to 35 minutes. Remove the baking sheet from the oven, sprinkle the peanuts with salt, carefully transfer to a serving bowl, and serve.

Almond Energy Bites

Maryellen loved to roller skate and swim. These healthy, portable, superpowered almond snacks could have given her energy on the go. Substitute peanut butter for almond butter, if you like, and choose whichever mix-ins appeal to you.

MAKES 18 BITES

1 cup rolled oats

⅔ cup almond butter, at room temperature

⅓ cup mini chocolate chips

⅓ cup ground flaxseed

¼ cup chopped toasted almonds

¼ cup honey

1 teaspoon vanilla extract

¼ teaspoon salt

½ cup toasted shredded coconut

 In a bowl, using a rubber spatula, stir together the oats, almond butter, mini chocolate chips, flaxseed, almonds, honey, vanilla, and salt until well combined. Cover the bowl with plastic wrap and refrigerate until the mixture has set, at least 30 minutes.

Pour the coconut into a shallow bowl. Scoop up a tablespoonful of the oat mixture and, using lightly dampened hands, shape the mixture into a ball. Place it on a large plate or cookie sheet. Repeat with the remaining mixture. Roll each ball in the coconut until evenly coated, then return the balls to the plate or cookie sheet.

Refrigerate until the balls are set, 5 to 10 minutes. Transfer to a serving plate and serve.

★ Meet Maryellen Larkin

Maryellen has a one-of-a-kind mind full of big, imaginative ideas. She lives in the suburbs of Daytona Beach, Florida, in the 1950s, where she longs to stand out. But in a family with five noisy siblings, she often gets lost in the shuffle. Helping with dinner prep and cleanup are some of the few times that Maryellen can talk to her mother by herself. As she tosses the salad or rinses the dishes, she loves being able to share her plans and ideas without a crowd drowning her out!

In Maryellen's Kitchen

In the 1950s, Americans were eager to buy new products like kitchen appliances, televisions, and cars—items that couldn't be purchased in the 1940s when factories were busy making airplanes to help fight World War II.

By the end of the war in 1945, Americans had been rationing goods like sugar, coffee, meat, butter, and milk for several years. In the 1950s, Americans rushed to buy new cooking gadgets and a wealth of ingredients now available to them. Convenience meals, like TV dinners, became popular for many families whose father and mother now worked full-time.

Popular Foods in Maryellen's Time

Fancy finger foods: There was a lot to celebrate in the 1950s and cocktail parties and themed parties were popular, with finger foods like crackers and cheese, pigs in a blanket, and meatballs.

Hearty main dishes: Meat and starch—like beef stroganoff, Salisbury steak, and meat loaf—were commonly found at the dinner table.

Cowboy cookies: These nutty oatmeal and chocolate chip cookies became popular as Americans, including Maryellen, started watching cowboy shows on television.

Homemade Fruit Leather

Living on a farm meant that Blaire had easy access to fresh fruit almost all year long. This recipe is a great way to use less-than-perfect fruit to create a snack to share with friends. Homemade fruit leather might seem like a lot of work, but as long as you keep a close eye on the fruit while it simmers, the rest of the work is hands-off. Plus, it's endlessly versatile!

MAKES 10 TO 12 FRUIT LEATHERS

1 pound chopped fresh fruit, such as peeled apples or pears, or peaches, plums, strawberries, blackberries, or raspberries

½ cup agave nectar or honey, plus more if needed

1 to 2 tablespoons fresh lemon juice

In a blender or food processor, combine the fruit, agave nectar, and 2 tablespoons lemon juice if using apples or pears, or 1 tablespoon lemon juice if using any other fruit. Blend until smooth. Taste and add more agave nectar, 1 tablespoon at a time, if the mixture needs to be sweeter.

Transfer the fruit purée to a saucepan. Set the pan over medium-high heat and bring the mixture to a simmer. Reduce the heat to medium-low and cook, stirring occasionally with a rubber spatula and scraping down the sides of the saucepan often, until the purée is very thick, 30 to 35 minutes. While the mixture is cooking, it will become foamy and start to bubble. If the bubbles become too big, or if the fruit starts to splatter, reduce the heat to low. As the purée thickens, stir often to prevent it from sticking or burning on the bottom of the pan. Remove the pan from the heat and let cool for 5 minutes.

Preheat the oven to 200°F. Line a cookie sheet with a silicone baking mat or nonstick aluminum foil.

~ *Continued on page 20* ~

~ Continued from page 19 ~

Using an icing spatula, spread the purée in a very thin layer on the prepared cookie sheet, leaving the edges slightly thicker to prevent them from burning. Bake until the purée is set and no longer sticky, about 3 hours. Check after 2 hours and again after 2½ hours. If the edges are starting to get very dark, turn off the oven and leave the cookie sheet in the warm oven for another hour until set.

Let the fruit leather cool completely on the cookie sheet on a wire rack. Lay a large sheet of waxed paper on a work surface. Peel the cooled fruit leather off the mat or foil and place it, smooth side down, on the waxed paper. Using scissors, trim off the excess waxed paper so that no paper extends beyond the edge of the fruit leather. Cut the fruit with the paper lengthwise into strips about 1 inch wide. Holding the waxed paper at the bottom of the strip, tightly roll up the fruit strips with the paper into coils. Carefully peel away the waxed paper before eating.

★ Meet Blaire Wilson

Blaire's family calls her a Mighty People Person. She can turn strangers into friends in a matter of minutes—something she does every day at the restaurant, inn, and farm her family runs. Blaire loves inventing new recipes with her mom, who is a professional chef. Seeing others enjoy what they've created is the most delicious part of cooking for Blaire.

In Blaire's Kitchen

When Blaire learns she's lactose intolerant, her whole world changes. Food used to be her way to bring people together, but now it makes her feel left out. It takes some trial and error to find the dairy substitutes she likes, but she eventually creates a gooey-good grilled soy cheese sandwich that hits the spot.

Food Substitutions

Today there are many options available for people with food allergies and sensitivities. Products that might not be available in a local grocery store can be purchased online. As Blaire discovers, being open to new tastes and textures makes eating exciting. To encourage others to try new foods, Blaire made cards with some of her favorite recipes and gave them to her friends.

Popular Foods in Blaire's Time

- Gluten-free products
- Cauliflower substitutes (pizza crust, rice, mashed potatoes)
- Local, organic produce
- Superfruits (acai, goji berries, mangosteens)
- Fermented foods (kombucha, kimchi, sauerkraut)

Jam Twists

You'd never guess that this spectacular-looking pastry is made from only four ingredients. You can use any flavor of jam you like, but tart-sweet lingonberry jam (available at specialty markets) is a celebrated product of Sweden and a favorite of Kirsten's. The puff-pastry twists that create a sunburst shape are also reminiscent of Kirsten's signature looped braids. For a special presentation, dust the cooled pastry with powdered sugar.

MAKES 6 TWISTS

All-purpose flour, for dusting

1 sheet (½ pound) frozen puff pastry, thawed

¼ cup berry jam, such as lingonberry, blueberry, cherry, or plum

1 large egg white

1 tablespoon turbinado sugar

Preheat the oven to 400°F. Line a cookie sheet with parchment paper.

Place the puff pastry on a lightly floured work surface, unfold, and press flat. Using a pizza cutter or a sharp knife, cut the sheet in half to make 2 rectangles. Spread the jam over 1 rectangle in an even layer. Place the other rectangle on top of the jam.

In a small bowl, using a fork, lightly beat the egg white. Using a pastry brush, lightly brush the top of the pastry with some of the egg white. Sprinkle half of the sugar evenly over the top, gently pressing the sugar into the dough so it adheres. Carefully turn the pastry over and brush the top side with the egg white. Sprinkle with the remaining sugar and gently press to adhere.

Using the pizza cutter or knife, cut the pastry rectangle lengthwise into 6 equal strips. Twist the ends of each strip in opposite directions to give the strip a spiraled look, then transfer the twists to the prepared cookie sheet, spacing them about 1½ inches apart. Refrigerate for 20 minutes.

Bake the pastry twists until they are puffed and golden and the jam is bubbling, about 15 minutes. Turn off the oven and leave the twists in the oven for 5 minutes longer to crisp. Remove the cookie sheet from the oven. Carefully transfer the twists to a wire rack and let cool briefly, then serve warm.

Spiced Applesauce Muffins

Plenty of spices amp up the flavor of these tender applesauce muffins, which are perfect for breakfast or a midday snack. During Kaya's time, the Nez Percé people lived throughout the Pacific Northwest, including present-day Washington. Today, Washington state is the largest producer of apples in the United States. If you want mini muffins, use a 24-cup mini muffin pan and decrease the cooking time by a few minutes.

MAKES 12 MUFFINS

Nonstick cooking spray

2 cups all-purpose flour

⅔ cup firmly packed light brown sugar

2 teaspoons baking powder

1 teaspoon ground cinnamon

1 teaspoon ground allspice

½ teaspoon salt

1 heaping cup applesauce

⅓ cup avocado or canola oil

1 large egg

Preheat the oven to 350°F. Spray a standard 12-cup muffin pan with nonstick cooking spray.

In a bowl, stir together the flour, sugar, baking powder, cinnamon, allspice, and salt. In another bowl, whisk together the applesauce, oil, and egg until smooth. Make a well in the center of the flour mixture and stir in the applesauce mixture just until evenly moistened. Divide the batter evenly among the prepared muffin cups, filling them about three-fourths full.

Bake until the muffins are golden and springy to the touch and a wooden skewer inserted into the center of a muffin comes out clean, 25 to 30 minutes. Remove the pan from the oven and set it on a wire rack. Let the muffins cool in the pan for 5 minutes, then transfer them to the rack and let cool slightly before serving. Serve warm or at room temperature.

★ Meet Kaya

In 1764, Kaya and her people live in harmony with nature. From the back of Kaya's beloved horse, Steps High, she can see the sheltering peaks of the Bitterroot Mountains. She hears the rushing waters of the river and the splash of salmon who offer themselves as food for her people, the Nimíipuu (who are today known as Nez Percé). When the snows move across the mountains, Kaya and her family move, too, following the seasons to gather food.

Kaya's Food Traditions

From spring through late fall, women and girls gathered all sorts of fresh berries and new roots. They dug bitterroots, kouse roots, and camas roots. Cornhusk bags worn on a strap across the body held the roots until they were ready for roasting.

Women and girls gathered huckleberries, serviceberries, and thimbleberries that grew along the mountainsides. Sturdy berry baskets had loops around their rims for easy carrying. Nimíipuu placed leaves atop the fruit in the baskets to keep the food fresh.

When the first roots and berries of the season were gathered, friends and family celebrated with feasting. They gave thanks to the Creator for these foods and honored the women and girls who gathered them.

Popular Foods in Kaya's Time

Camas: One of the most important foods in the Nimíipuu diet, this bulb was harvested in the summer, then baked in a pit, dried, ground, and made into dough for camas cakes.

Huckleberries: Wild berries were a staple of the Nimíipuu diet and were eaten both fresh and dried. Wild huckleberries were the most popular and abundant berries.

Salmon: Nimíipuu began fishing salmon early in the spring and followed the salmon runs until fall. They ate fresh salmon while it was available and preserved hundreds of pounds for winter storage. Men were responsible for catching salmon, while women would clean, cut, and dry them.

Cosmos Doughnuts

Creative and artistic Luciana has a swirl of purple in her hair, much like the swirls of colorful icing atop these whimsical chocolate cake doughnuts. When frying doughnuts, make sure there's an adult nearby, and never overcrowd the pan. Decorate these with star-shaped, multicolored sprinkles, or dust with edible glitter for a truly out-of-this-world effect.

MAKES 10 DOUGHNUTS

CAKE DOUGHNUTS

1 cup all-purpose flour, plus flour for dusting

1 cup cake flour

¼ cup unsweetened natural cocoa powder

1 teaspoon baking powder

½ teaspoon baking soda

½ teaspoon salt

1 large egg

½ cup sugar

½ cup buttermilk

1 tablespoon unsalted butter, melted

1 teaspoon vanilla extract

Canola or peanut oil for deep-frying

To make the doughnuts, in a medium bowl, sift together the all-purpose flour, cake flour, cocoa powder, baking powder, baking soda, and salt. In a large bowl, using an electric mixer, beat the egg and sugar on low speed until creamy and pale, about 2 minutes. Add the buttermilk, melted butter, and vanilla and beat until blended. Add the flour mixture and beat just until the mixture comes together into a soft dough. Cover the bowl with plastic wrap and refrigerate the dough until firm, at least 30 minutes or up to 1 hour.

Line a cookie sheet with paper towels. Pour oil into a deep-fryer or a deep, heavy-bottomed sauté pan to a depth of 2 inches and warm over medium-high heat until it registers 360°F on a deep-frying thermometer.

On a generously floured work surface, roll out the dough into a round 10 inches in diameter and ½ inch thick. Using a 3-inch round doughnut cutter, cut out as many doughnuts and holes as possible. Gather up the dough scraps, press them together, roll them out again, and cut out more doughnuts.

Using a slotted or skimmer spoon, carefully lower 2 to 5 doughnuts and holes into the hot oil and deep-fry until dark brown and crusty on the first side, about 1½ minutes. Turn the doughnuts and holes over and fry until dark brown and crusty on the second side, about 1 minute longer. Transfer to the prepared cookie sheet. Repeat to fry the remaining doughnuts and holes, allowing the oil to return to 360°F between batches.

~ Continued on page 28 ~

~ *Continued from page 27* ~

VANILLA GLAZE

6 tablespoons (¾ stick) unsalted butter, melted

2½ cups powdered sugar

5 tablespoons hot water, plus more if needed

1 teaspoon vanilla extract

Pink, blue, and purple gel food coloring

Edible glitter and/or edible silver star sprinkles for decorating (optional)

To make the glaze, in a bowl, whisk together the melted butter, sugar, hot water, and vanilla until smooth. Whisk in 1 to 2 teaspoons more hot water if needed to give the glaze a smooth consistency.

Divide the glaze evenly between 2 bowls. Dip a toothpick into the pink food coloring, then dip the coloring into a bowl of glaze. Dip a clean toothpick into the blue food coloring, then dip the coloring into the same bowl. Do the same with another clean toothpick and the purple food coloring. Then use the toothpick to gently swirl the food colorings into the glaze and create color streaks. Don't swirl the toothpick too much or the colors will blend together. Repeat this process with the second bowl of glaze.

Dip the top of a doughnut into the glaze and, as you lift the doughnut out of the glaze, gently twist it to let any excess glaze drip off. Place the doughnut, glaze side up, on a platter and sprinkle with edible glitter and/or stars (if using). Repeat with the remaining doughnuts and the holes. When the first bowl of glaze no longer has colored swirls, or if the colors have started to blend together too much, use the other bowl of glaze. Let the glaze set for 10 minutes, then serve.

★ Meet Luciana Vega

Luciana's over the moon when she gets accepted into Space Camp, a big step toward reaching her dream of becoming an astronaut, and the first kid on Mars. Her family's roots are in Chile, South America, where the red desert landscape looks just like Mars. On a 2018 visit to see her family in Chile (Luciana has 15 cousins!), everyone pitches in to make piles of tamales for a big party. At Space Camp, Luciana learns what foods astronauts eat in space, and they're about as far from tamales as you can get!

Space Foods

In space, astronauts eat from a menu they've selected several months before the flight. This includes a combination of frozen and fresh foods that provide a wealth of vitamins and minerals, such as fruits, nuts, chicken, beef, seafood, and sweets. Things like entrées, salads, soups, and desserts come in single-service containers that are disposed of after every meal.

Chilean Foods

Before the Spanish came to Chile, foods like potatoes, corn, beans, and seafood were everyday staples. With the arrival of Spanish colonizers came new foods such as wheat, beef, and poultry. Today, classic Chilean dishes include curanto, empanadas, and ceviche.

Bacon: From breakfast to dessert, bacon flavors everything from ice cream and doughnuts to Thanksgiving turkeys.

Sweet salsas: Since the early 2000s, sweet fruit salsas with a hit of hot chiles have become more popular, topping everything from fish tacos to desserts.

Ice Cream Sandwiches

During World War II, ice cream was often given to soldiers as a treat to boost morale. It was also a favorite of Molly and her friends. Choose whatever flavor you'd like to smoosh between the dark chocolate cookies: vanilla, coffee, strawberry, or mint chip. If you like, roll the edges of the assembled sandwiches in chopped toasted peanuts or mini chocolate chips before freezing.

MAKES 6 ICE CREAM SANDWICHES

1¼ cups firmly packed dark brown sugar

½ cup (1 stick) unsalted butter, plus butter for greasing

3 ounces unsweetened chocolate, coarsely chopped

1 large egg

2 teaspoons vanilla extract

1¼ cups all-purpose flour

¾ teaspoon baking soda

¼ teaspoon salt

1½ cups semisweet chocolate chips

1½ pints ice cream, such as vanilla or chocolate, slightly softened

 Preheat the oven to 350°F. Lightly butter 2 cookie sheets.

In a heavy saucepan over low heat, combine the brown sugar, butter, and chopped chocolate. Heat, stirring often, until the chocolate and butter melts. Transfer the mixture to a large bowl and let cool to lukewarm. Add the flour mixture to the chocolate mixture and whisk until smooth. In another bowl, whisk together the flour, baking soda, and salt. Add the dry ingredients to the chocolate mixture and stir until blended. Stir in the chocolate chips. Cover the bowl with plastic wrap and refrigerate until firm, about 30 minutes.

Drop the dough by generous tablespoonfuls onto the prepared cookie sheets, spacing the cookies at least 3 inches apart. You should have 12 cookies. With dampened fingers, smooth the cookies into slightly flattened rounds about 3 inches in diameter. Bake the cookies until the edges darken and the centers are still slightly soft, about 10 minutes. Remove the cookie sheet from the oven and set it on a wire rack. Let cool for 5 minutes, then use a metal spatula to move the cookies directly to the rack. Let cool completely.

Lay half of the cookies, flat side up, on a work surface. Spread about ½ cup of the ice cream on each cookie, then top the ice cream with 1 of the remaining cookies, flat side down. Smooth out the sides using a small icing spatula and wrap each sandwich in plastic wrap. Lay on a clean, dry cookie sheet and freeze until firm, at least 2 hours or up to 3 days.

Peanut Butter–Chocolate Buckeyes

Buckeyes are a much-loved treat in Cincinnati, Ohio, where Kit and her family lived. Made by dipping a peanut butter filling in chocolate, they resemble the nuts from the state tree of Ohio, the Ohio buckeye tree. Save any leftover chocolate shell to pour over ice cream, where it will harden into a crunchy treat.

MAKES ABOUT 40 BUCKEYES

BUCKEYES

1 cup smooth peanut butter

2 cups powdered sugar

1 tablespoon
unsalted butter

1 teaspoon vanilla extract

CHOCOLATE SHELL

½ pound bittersweet
chocolate, roughly chopped

1 cup vegetable shortening

½ cup light corn syrup

Flaky sea salt

To make the buckeyes, line a cookie sheet with parchment paper. In a large bowl, using an electric mixer, beat the peanut butter, powdered sugar, butter, and vanilla on medium speed until smooth. Scoop the mixture into balls the size of a rounded tablespoon and and place on the prepared cookie sheet. Refrigerate the balls while you make the chocolate shell.

To make the chocolate shell, in a saucepan, combine the chocolate, shortening, and corn syrup. Set the pan over low heat and heat, stirring occasionally, until the chocolate is melted and the mixture is smooth. Remove from the heat and let cool to room temperature

Line another cookie sheet with parchment paper. Using a wooden skewer, dip the peanut butter balls one at a time into the chocolate, then return them to the cookie sheet. Sprinkle each cookie with salt. Freeze the buckeyes for at least 30 minutes before serving.

Ice Cream Bonbons

Ice cream was invented in Philadelphia around the same time that Addy lived there. Philly-style ice cream is lighter than custard-style ice cream, and it doesn't contain eggs. For an authentic touch, choose vanilla-bean ice cream for this recipe, the most popular flavor of that time!

MAKES ABOUT 25 BONBONS

1 pint vanilla bean ice cream, preferably Philadelphia style

1 (12-ounce) bag semisweet chocolate chips

2 tablespoons coconut oil or vegetable shortening

¼ cup rainbow or white nonpareils

Place a rimmed baking sheet in the freezer until cold, about 20 minutes.

Using a small ice cream scoop, scoop out small balls of ice cream (each about 1 inch in diameter) and place them on the chilled baking sheet. Cover with plastic wrap and freeze until very cold, 6 to 8 hours.

In a microwave-safe bowl, combine the chocolate chips and oil. Microwave on high, stirring every 20 seconds, just until the mixture is melted and smooth. Let cool for 5 to 7 minutes.

Put the nonpareils in a small bowl. Using a wooden skewer and a fork, and working quickly, skewer an ice cream ball, dip it into the chocolate to cover it completely, then dip the bonbon into the nonpareils, covering it about halfway. Use the fork to push the bonbon from the skewer onto the cold baking sheet. Repeat with the rest of the ice cream balls, spacing them slightly apart on the baking sheet. Freeze until the ice cream is solid and the chocolate is set before serving, at least 2 hours, or transfer to a large covered container and freeze for up to 2 weeks.

Moon Pies

Luciana dreams of traveling through space, becoming the first girl to explore Mars. These full-moon-shaped pies would be a terrific treat to bring along on a big adventure. Prepared with homemade graham cookies sandwiched with gooey marshmallow crème, the pies are dipped in dark-as-night chocolate. They take time to put together but are totally worth it.

MAKES ABOUT 15 MOON PIES

GRAHAM COOKIES

1 cup finely ground graham cracker crumbs (about 6 whole crackers)

1 cup all-purpose flour, plus flour for dusting

½ teaspoon baking powder

½ teaspoon ground cinnamon

½ teaspoon salt

½ cup (1 stick) unsalted butter, at room temperature

½ cup firmly packed dark brown sugar

1 large egg

1 teaspoon vanilla extract

2 tablespoons whole milk

About 1¾ cups marshmallow crème

CHOCOLATE COATING

2⅔ cups semisweet chocolate chips

2 tablespoons vegetable oil

To make the cookies, in a medium bowl, stir together the graham cracker crumbs, flour, baking powder, cinnamon, and salt. In a large bowl, using an electric mixer, beat the butter and sugar on medium-high speed until light and fluffy, about 1 minute. Add the egg and vanilla and beat until blended. Turn off the mixer and scrape down the bowl with a rubber spatula. Add the graham cracker mixture and beat on low speed until combined. Add the milk and beat just until the dough comes together. Transfer the dough to a clean work surface and press into a thick disk. Wrap the disk in plastic wrap and refrigerate for at least 1 hour or up to overnight.

Preheat the oven to 350°F. Line 2 cookie sheets with parchment paper.

On a lightly floured surface, roll out the dough into a round about ⅛ inch thick. Using a fluted 2¾-inch round cookie cutter, cut out as many cookies as possible. Transfer the cookies to the prepared cookie sheets, spacing them at least 1 inch apart. Gather up the dough scraps, press them together, roll them out again, and cut out more cookies. You should have about 30 cookies.

Bake 1 cookie sheet at a time until the cookies are lightly golden around the edges, about 13 minutes. Remove the cookie sheet from the oven and set it on a wire rack. Let cool for 5 minutes, then use a metal spatula to move

～ Continued on page 36 ～

~ *Continued from page 35* ~

the cookies directly to the rack and let cool completely. Repeat to bake the rest of the cookies. Turn half of the cookies bottom side up. Dollop about 2 tablespoons marshmallow crème onto the center of each overturned cookie. Top with a second cookie, bottom side down, and press the top cookie gently so the crème fills the sandwich. Place the filled cookies on a cookie sheet, cover with plastic wrap, and place in the freezer to firm up, at least 20 minutes or up to overnight.

To make the coating, in a small saucepan, pour water to a depth of about 1 inch. Set the pan over medium-low heat and bring to a gentle simmer. Rest a bowl on the saucepan so that it is over (but not touching) the water. Add the chocolate chips to the bowl and heat, stirring occasionally with a rubber spatula, until the chocolate is melted and is smooth. Remove the bowl from the heat and let cool slightly, then stir in the oil. Let cool for about 5 minutes.

To coat the moon pies, place a wire rack on a cookie sheet. Immerse a chilled moon pie into the melted chocolate and use 2 forks to maneuver it so it is evenly coated. Transfer to the wire rack. Repeat with the remaining moon pies. Refrigerate the moon pies until the chocolate hardens, at least 30 minutes. Serve chilled or at room temperature.

Southern Tea Cakes

Addy tried these tender cake-like cookies for the first time at a church supper in Philadelphia. Buttermilk gives this updated version a cakelike texture, and plenty of lemon zest and juice and juice add a zingy flavor. Many traditional recipes for tea cakes use molasses to flavor the cookies; this version swaps in sugar.

MAKES ABOUT 48 COOKIES

2 cups all-purpose flour, plus flour for dusting

¾ teaspoon baking soda

½ teaspoon kosher salt

¾ cup (1½ sticks) unsalted butter, at room temperature

1 cup sugar

1 large egg

2 tablespoons finely grated lemon zest

3 tablespoons buttermilk

1 teaspoon fresh lemon juice

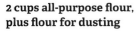

In a medium bowl, whisk together the flour, baking soda, and salt. Set aside. In a large bowl, using an electric mixer, beat the butter and sugar on medium-high speed until light and fluffy, 2 to 3 minutes. Add the egg and lemon zest and beat on low speed until the egg is incorporated. On low speed, mix in the dry ingredients. Add the buttermilk and lemon juice and beat until just incorporated.

Sprinkle a work surface with flour. Transfer the dough to the floured surface. Form the dough into an even log about 12 inches long. Wrap tightly in parchment paper and refrigerate until firm, at least 3 hours or up to overnight.

Position 2 racks in the oven so that they are evenly space apart and preheat the oven to 350°F. Line 2 cookie sheets with parchment paper.

Unwrap the chilled dough and slice into rounds ½ inch thick. Arrange the rounds on the prepared cookie sheets, spacing them about 1 inch apart.

Bake until the edges are lightly golden, about 12 minutes, rotating the cookie sheets from front to back and between the racks. Let the cookies cool on the sheets for 5 minutes, then use a metal spatula to move the cookies directly to a wire rack. Let cool completely.

Savory Shareables

Sweet Potato Chips

Potato chips gained widespread popularity in the 1920s, and they would be a terrific snack to eat while watching baseball, one of Kit's favorite pastimes. This version makes use of healthy and economical sweet potatoes, but virtually any root vegetable works well in this recipe: potatoes, parsnips, beets, or carrots would all be fun to experiment with.

MAKES 2 SERVINGS

1 small (¼ pound) sweet potato, peeled

1 tablespoon olive oil

Salt

Preheat the oven to 400°F. Line a cookie sheet with parchment paper.

Using a food processor fitted with the thinnest slicing disk, or using a mandoline or a sharp knife, have an adult help you carefully slice the sweet potato crosswise into very thin rounds no more than ⅛ inch thick.

Put the slices in a large bowl and drizzle with the oil. Gently toss the slices until evenly coated. Spread the sweet potato slices in a single layer, overlapping them as little as possible, on the prepared cookie sheet. Use a pastry brush to spread the oil remaining in the bowl on any uncoated slices.

Bake the for 10 minutes, then turn the slices using a spatula and sprinkle them evenly with ¼ teaspoon salt. Return the cookie sheet to the oven and continue to bake until the slices are dry and some are lightly browned, about 10 minutes longer. Be sure to check the chips often during the last few minutes of baking so they don't burn.

Remove the cookie sheet from the oven. Transfer the chips to a serving bowl. Sprinkle with a little more salt and serve warm.

Cheese & Chive Crackers

Courtney and her best friend, Sarah, like to hang out at the mall after school—a popular 1980s pastime. First stop: a snack from the food court. These savory cheese crackers make a terrific bite-size treat.

MAKES ABOUT 2 DOZEN CRACKERS

2 cups shredded Comté or Gruyère cheese

½ cup grated Parmesan cheese

6 tablespoons (¾ stick) unsalted butter

1 cup all-purpose flour

Pinch of cayenne pepper

3 tablespoons finely chopped fresh chives

Coarse sea salt

 In a food processor, combine the Comté and Parmesan cheeses, the butter, flour, and cayenne and process until well combined and crumbly, 40 to 60 seconds. Transfer the mixture to the center of a large piece of plastic wrap. Shape the mixture into a log about 2 inches in diameter and 6 to 7 inches long. Roll up the log in the plastic wrap, patting it to form a smooth, even cylinder. Refrigerate for at least 1 hour or up to overnight.

Preheat the oven to 350°F. Line 2 cookie sheets with parchment paper.

Unwrap the chilled dough and slice into rounds about ¼ inch thick. Arrange the rounds on the prepared cookie sheets, spacing them about 2 inches apart. Sprinkle the rounds evenly with the chives and top each with a pinch of salt.

Bake 1 cookie sheet at a time until the crackers are light golden brown, 10 to 15 minutes, rotating the pan front to back halfway through baking. For crispier crackers, bake for up to 3 minutes longer, watching carefully to prevent overbrowning. Remove the cookie sheet from the oven and serve the crackers right away. Repeat to bake the rest of the crackers.

⭐ Meet Courtney Moore

Courtney's a totally rad California girl living in the 1980s. She loves music, movies, and the mall. Her parents are divorced, and Courtney spends every weekend at her dad's apartment. That's where she and her best friend, Sarah, have sleepovers, complete with rented movies and microwave popcorn. The next morning, Courtney's dad cooks homemade waffles for them.

In Courtney's Kitchen

Both Courtney's mom and her stepdad, Mike, worked, so Courtney and her stepsister, Tina, hung out at home alone after school. When Courtney's mom decided to run for mayor, the whole family had to pitch in and help with chores around the house—including dinner prep. Courtney and Tina set the table while Mike heated up a casserole, made macaroni and cheese from a box mix, or ordered a pizza.

School lunch: Running for mayor meant Mom was extra busy, so Courtney started packing her own lunch every night before going to bed. She usually made a bologna or peanut butter sandwich, put some cheese balls in a baggie, and added a prepackaged cookie or brownie to her lunch box.

Malls: Inside America's giant malls, food courts offered endless choices. Shoppers could grab a snack or have a meal. Mike ran an electronics store in Orange Valley mall, so Courtney's family often met at the food court for a quick week-night dinner.

Making dinner: In the 1980s, many American kids were growing up in single-parent families or in homes where both parents worked. Grocery stores were full of frozen foods, box mixes, and fully cooked meats that made meal prep fast and convenient. Drive-through lanes at fast food restaurants were also popular.

Foods in Courtney's Time

Because microwaves were so popular, microwavable snacks were a big fixture in the 1980s. Snacks like Pizza Rolls™ and Hot Pockets™ were enjoyed at birthday parties and after-school gatherings. Convenience foods like Lunchables™ were also kid favorites.

Garden Caprese Tomatoes with Pesto

Melody loved the calm peacefulness of working in the garden, and one of her favorite things to grow were juicy summer tomatoes. This recipe is a beautiful way to showcase tomatoes—thick slices of creamy fresh mozzarella cheese are tucked into each tomato, creating a dramatic effect. Topped with a basil pesto vinaigrette, this makes a terrific appetizer, light lunch, or side dish.

MAKES 4 SERVINGS

1 large ball (8 ounces) fresh mozzarella cheese

4 medium ripe tomatoes

¼ cup store-bought basil pesto

1 tablespoon red wine vinegar

¼ cup olive oil

Salt and ground black pepper

Cut the ball of mozzarella in half lengthwise, then cut each half crosswise into 10 thin slices. Set aside.

Using a sharp knife, cut around the stem of each tomato to remove the core; discard the core. Place the tomatoes, cored side down, on a cutting board. Using a sharp knife, make 5 evenly spaced cuts in each tomato without cutting all the way through.

Insert 1 slice of mozzarella into each cut, aligning it as much as possible with the sides of the tomato. Place each mozzarella-stuffed tomato on a plate.

In a bowl, whisk together the pesto and vinegar. Add the oil in a thin stream, whisking constantly until the vinaigrette is well blended.

Drizzle the vinaigrette over the mozzarella-stuffed tomatoes. Season to taste with salt and pepper and serve.

Mac-&-Cheese Cups

Boxed macaroni and cheese was first introduced during the Great Depression. It was an inexpensive way to feed the entire family or a crowd of hungry boarders. These mac-and-cheese cups can be made in individual portions or as a family-style dinner. For a new spin on an old favorite, stir in chopped blanched broccoli, spinach, or sautéed mushrooms and leeks.

MAKES 6 SERVINGS

MAC AND CHEESE

3½ cups macaroni

1 tablespoon olive oil

Nonstick cooking spray

3 tablespoons unsalted butter

3 tablespoons all-purpose flour

1¾ cups whole milk, warmed

1¾ cups shredded white Cheddar cheese

Salt and ground black pepper

CRUNCHY TOPPING

¾ cup shredded white Cheddar cheese

½ cup panko bread crumbs

1 tablespoon unsalted butter, melted

To make the mac and cheese, fill a large saucepan three-fourths full of salted water. Set the pan over high heat and bring the water to a boil. Add the pasta and boil until the pasta is almost cooked through but still slightly firm, about 5 minutes. Drain in a large colander set in the sink. Rinse under cold running water, drizzle with the oil, and toss to mix. Set aside.

Preheat the oven to 375°F. Spray six 6–fl oz ramekins or an 8-inch square baking dish with nonstick cooking spray and place on a cookie sheet.

Return the saucepan to medium-low heat and melt the butter. Add the flour and milk and cook, stirring, until thickened, about 3 minutes. Add the cheese and stir until melted and hot. Stir in ¼ teaspoon salt and a generous pinch of pepper. Pour the pasta into the cheese mixture and stir to combine. Divide the macaroni and cheese evenly among the prepared ramekins or pour it into the baking dish.

To make the topping, in a bowl, stir together the cheese, bread crumbs, and melted butter. Sprinkle the topping evenly over the top of the ramekins or the baking dish.

Bake until the cheese is bubbling and lightly browned on top, about 20 minutes. Remove the cookie sheet with the ramekins or baking dish from the oven and let cool briefly before serving. Serve hot.

⭐ Meet Kit Kittredge

Kit has a nose for news, and when she sees how the Depression is affecting people around her, she wants to know what's going on. After Kit's dad loses his job, it's their family that's facing hard times. When her mother gets the idea to turn their home into a boarding house, Kit's not too thrilled with the changes—and especially the extra chores. Cooking for five more people is a lot of work. But to Kit's surprise, having a houseful turns out to be a lot of fun, too.

In Kit's Kitchen

Families had to learn how to stretch their dollars as far as possible, so they purchased cheaper ingredients and relied on inexpensive foods like soup, beans, and oatmeal.

Gardens: Like many families, the Kittredges planted a garden in their yard. They enjoyed fresh vegetables in the summer and canned or preserved produce to eat during the winter. Kit's family even raised chickens in their yard. Eggs were a staple ingredient for many dishes and could be sold to the neighbors for extra money.

Making do: A popular phrase in the 1940s was "use it up, wear it out, make it do, or do without." The Depression forced people to find new ways to make the most of what they had—whether it was food, clothing, or money. But hard times also encouraged people to be creative and resourceful and appreciate the little luxuries of life—and especially the people in it. They also made use of leftovers and ingredients in new and inventive ways—like turning stale bread into bread pudding or bruised apples into applesauce.

Popular Foods in Kit's Time

- Chili
- Macaroni and cheese (Kraft Mac and Cheese)
- Soups and beans
- Creamed chicken or chipped beef on biscuits or toast

- Casseroles
- Spam
- Pies: Hot water pie, vinegar pie, and sugar pie
- Puddings: Bread pudding, baked apple pudding

Savory Ranch Popcorn

Creamy herbed ranch dressing was invented in the 1950s but surged to popularity in the 1980s when it was used as a dressing, topping, or dip for just about everything. Courtney and her friend Sarah love watching movies, and eating popcorn is part of the fun. Toss the popcorn with the seasonings when hot and just popped for the best results.

MAKES 4 TO 6 SERVINGS

3 tablespoons canola oil

½ cup popcorn kernels

2 tablespoons unsalted butter, melted

2 tablespoons grated Parmesan cheese

½ teaspoon onion powder

½ teaspoon dried dill

½ teaspoon salt

¼ teaspoon garlic powder

In a large, heavy-bottomed pan with a tight-fitting lid, warm the oil and 3 popcorn kernels over medium heat. Add the rest of the popcorn in an even layer and cover the pan. Leave the pan untouched until you hear the first few pops, then shake the pan and continue to cook, shaking the pan every 20 seconds or so, until the popping slows way, way down, about 6 minutes. Remove from the heat.

In a large bowl, stir together the melted butter and cheese. Add the onion powder, dill, salt, and garlic powder. Add the hot popcorn and toss to mix. Serve right away.

Fresh Peach Salsa with Star Chips

When summer peaches are ripe, make this simple but delicious salsa, perfect as a topping for grilled chicken or fish or for sharing with a big bowl of chips. The easy-to-make star chips are reminiscent of one of Luciana's prized possessions: her star necklace, which was given to her on her first birthday. She wore it only for special occasions.

MAKES 4 TO 6 SERVINGS

PEACH SALSA

2 ripe but slightly firm peaches, pitted and diced

3 tablespoons minced red onion

3 tablespoons finely chopped fresh cilantro

½ to 1½ teaspoons minced canned chipotle chile in adobo sauce (optional)

1 teaspoon fresh lime juice

Salt and ground black pepper

STAR CHIPS

6 (6-inch) corn tortillas

Canola oil, for greasing

To make the salsa, in a bowl, stir together the peaches, red onion, cilantro, chile (if using), and lime juice. Season to taste with salt and pepper. Cover and let stand at room temperature for at least 30 minutes or up to 3 hours.

To make the star chips, preheat the oven to 350°F.

Using a 3-inch star-shaped cookie cutter, cut stars out of each corn tortilla (you should get 3 from each tortilla). Lightly grease 2 cookie sheets with oil, then place the stars on the cookie sheets so that they are not overlapping.

Bake until the chips are brown around the edges, 8 to 10 minutes. Let the chips cool slightly, then transfer to a platter and and serve with the salsa.

Cheese Fondue

A warm pot of gooey fondue—either cheese or chocolate—is the ultimate shareable party food, and it was extremely popular in the 1970s. Julie's favorite food was chocolate fondue, but she was equally happy with the savory cheese version like the one here. Bread is a quick and favored dipper, but blanched crisp-tender broccoli and cauliflower florets are also delicious.

MAKES 8 SERVINGS

About 2 cups shredded Gruyère cheese

About 2 cups shredded Emmentaler, Swiss, or fontina cheese

2 tablespoons cornstarch

½ clove garlic

½ cup low-sodium vegetable or chicken broth

3 tablespoons cider vinegar

1 or 2 loaves French bread, cut into 1-inch cubes

 Place the Gruyère and Emmentaler cheeses in a large bowl, add the cornstarch, and toss until the cheese shreds are evenly coated. Rub the cut side of the garlic clove around the inside of a fondue pot; discard the garlic.

Pour the broth, vinegar, and ½ cup water into the fondue pot. Set the pot over medium-high heat and bring just to a boil. Reduce the heat to medium and whisk a handful of the cheese mixture into the broth mixture until it is almost melted. Repeat with the remaining cheese mixture in about four batches. Continue whisking until the cheese is completely melted and the fondue bubbles, about 1 minute longer.

Set the pot over Sterno or another heat source to keep warm. Put the bread in a basket and place alongside the pot. Use fondue forks to dip pieces of the bread into the fondue.

"Cheesy" Kale Chips

Ever since the early 2000s, the craze for kale seems never-ending. Plus, kale is one of the easiest crops you can grow in your garden or on a sustainable farm. Nutritional yeast creates a "cheesy" flavor without the use of dairy, perfect for anyone who is lactose intolerant like Blaire.

MAKES 6 TO 8 SERVINGS

1 bunch curly kale (about 10 ounces), ribs removed and leaves torn into 3-inch by 1 inch, then drained

½ cup raw cashews, soaked for 1 hour in hot water to cover by an inch, and drained

⅓ cup nutritional yeast

2 tablespoons olive oil

1 tablespoon low-sodium soy sauce

1 tablespoon fresh lemon juice

¼ teaspoon salt

¼ teaspoon garlic powder

Position 3 racks in the oven so that they are evenly spaced and preheat the oven to 200°F. Line 3 rimmed baking sheets with parchment paper.

Fill a large bowl with water and add the kale, stirring it around with your hands to loosen any dirt. Drain the kale in a colander set in the sink. Repeat until you don't see any more dirt in the water, then dry the kale thoroughly in a salad spinner.

In a small food processor, combine the cashews, nutritional yeast, oil, soy sauce, lemon juice, salt, and garlic powder. Process until a thick, rough paste forms. Place the kale in a large bowl and add the cashew mixture. Using your hands, massage the cashew mixture into the kale leaves until it is evenly distributed, about 5 minutes. Be sure to check for any hidden blobs of paste in the leaves. Spread the kale leaves in a single layer, without touching, the prepared baking sheets, dividing them evenly.

Bake, rotating the baking sheets to different racks every 30 minutes, until the leaves are crispy and lightly browned, 1 hour 45 minutes to 2 hours. Be sure to check on the kale chips often toward the end of baking so they don't burn.

Remove the baking sheets from the oven and set them on wire racks. Let the chips cool completely. Pile onto a serving plate or in a shallow serving bowl and serve.

Potato Latkes

Rebecca's Jewish family traditionally served potato latkes to celebrate Hanukkah.
Fried until browned and crisp, they are served with sour cream and applesauce on top.
This gluten-free version uses almond flour, but feel free to substitute all-purpose
flour or matzo meal. Make sure to dry the shredded potatoes well.

MAKES 4 SERVINGS

1 pound russet potatoes, peeled, or ½ pound *each* russet potatoes and sweet potatoes, peeled

3 large eggs, lightly beaten

¾ cup almond flour

⅓ cup minced fresh flat-leaf parsley

2 cloves garlic, minced

1 teaspoon salt

½ teaspoon ground black pepper

2 tablespoons canola or avocado oil, plus more if needed

½ cup sour cream

½ cup applesauce

 Using the large holes on a box grater-shredder, shred the potatoes. Using a paper towel or a salad spinner, blot the shredded potatoes dry. In a large bowl, combine the shredded potatoes, eggs, almond flour, parsley, garlic, salt, and pepper and mix with a rubber spatula until well combined.

Preheat the oven to 200°F.

In a large nonstick frying pan over medium heat, warm the oil, swirling to coat the pan. Scoop up ¼ cup of the potato mixture and, using your hands, form it into a ¼-inch-thick round. Carefully place the latke in the pan and repeat to make more latkes, shaping only as many as will comfortably fit in a single layer in the pan. Cook, without pressing on or moving the latkes, until lightly browned on the bottoms, about 3 minutes. Using a wide spatula, flip each latke and continue to cook until lightly browned on the second side, about 3 minutes. Transfer to a cookie sheet and keep warm in the oven. Repeat with the remaining potato mixture, adding more oil to the pan as needed before cooking each batch.

Set out the sour cream and applesauce in serving bowls. Arrange the warm latkes on a platter and serve right away.

Deviled Eggs

Deviled eggs were very much in vogue in the 1970s, the perfect finger food for a party and a great snack for athletic girls on the go like Julie. For an elegant, party-ready presentation, use a pastry bag fitted with a star-shaped tip to pipe the yolk filling into the egg whites. Personalize the eggs by adding a teaspoon of minced fresh parsley, some finely grated lemon zest, or a spoonful of minced bread and butter pickles to the filling.

MAKES 4 SERVINGS

6 large eggs

3 tablespoons mayonnaise

1 teaspoon Dijon mustard

Salt and ground black pepper

½ teaspoon sweet paprika

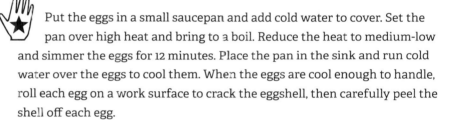 Put the eggs in a small saucepan and add cold water to cover. Set the pan over high heat and bring to a boil. Reduce the heat to medium-low and simmer the eggs for 12 minutes. Place the pan in the sink and run cold water over the eggs to cool them. When the eggs are cool enough to handle, roll each egg on a work surface to crack the eggshell, then carefully peel the shell off each egg.

Place the eggs on a cutting board, then cut each egg in half lengthwise. Using a small spoon, scoop out the yolks and place them in a bowl.

Add the mayonnaise and mustard to the bowl with the yolks. Use the spoon to mash them all together into a smooth paste. Season to taste with salt and pepper.

Carefully scoop a small mound of the yolk mixture back into each egg white half. Arrange the deviled eggs on a plate, sprinkle each with a pinch of paprika, and serve.

Chile-Corn Muffins

New Mexican cuisine is a blend of Spanish, Native American, and Mexican food and techniques. Green chiles are a common ingredient and can be found in everything from sauces and salsa to meaty green chili and breads. They would have been a common ingredient used in colonial New Mexico foods when Josefina was growing up. Moist and rich, these savory muffins are ideal served warm from the oven. Look for roasted, peeled, and diced green chiles in cans at most markets.

MAKES 12 MUFFINS

Nonstick cooking spray

¾ cup fine cornmeal

¾ cup all-purpose flour

2 teaspoons baking powder

1½ teaspoons chili powder

½ teaspoon baking soda

½ teaspoon salt

¾ cup sour cream

2 large eggs

4 tablespoons (½ stick) unsalted butter, melted

½ cup finely shredded Cheddar cheese

¼ cup diced roasted green chiles

¼ cup corn kernels

Preheat the oven to 400°F. Spray a standard 12-cup muffin pan with nonstick cooking spray.

In a large bowl, whisk together the cornmeal, flour, baking powder, chili powder, baking soda, and salt. Set aside. In a medium bowl, whisk together the sour cream, eggs, and melted butter until smooth. Stir in the cheese, chiles, and corn kernels. Add the sour cream mixture to the flour mixture and stir just until the batter is blended. Divide the batter evenly among the prepared muffin cups, filling them about two-thirds full.

Bake until a wooden skewer inserted into the center of a muffin comes out clean, about 15 minutes. Remove the pan from the oven and set it on a wire rack. Let the muffins cool in the pan for 5 minutes, then transfer them directly to the rack. Serve warm or at room temperature.

Hummus with Victory Garden Veggie Dippers

Planting a victory garden not only boosted morale for Molly, her family, and others, but they were also an important means for making sure healthy vegetables were on the table during World War II. Paired with creamy, homemade hummus—easier than you think!—this recipe makes great use of vegetables that can easily be grown in a home garden: radishes, carrots, and beets. Other vegetables, like zucchini and cucumbers, also work well.

MAKES 4 TO 6 SERVINGS

VEGGIE DIPPERS

2 watermelon radishes, peeled

2 large rainbow carrots, peeled

1 small golden beet, peeled

HUMMUS

2 (15-ounce) cans chickpeas, drained and rinsed

½ cup fresh lemon juice, plus more if needed

½ cup tahini

3 tablespoons olive oil

3 cloves garlic, minced

¼ teaspoon ground cumin

Salt

Fill a large bowl with ice water. Using a food processor fitted with the thinnest slicing disk, or using a mandoline or a sharp knife, have an adult help you carefully slice the radishes, carrots, and beet crosswise into very thin rounds. As the slices are cut, transfer them to the ice water. Let the vegetables stand in the water for at least 20 minutes, or cover the bowl and refrigerate for up to 1 day.

To make the hummus, in a food processor, combine the chickpeas, lemon juice, tahini, oil, garlic, cumin, and ¾ teaspoon salt. Process to a very smooth purée. Taste and adjust the seasoning with salt and lemon juice if needed.

Transfer the hummus to a serving bowl set on a plate. Drain the vegetables, pat dry with a paper towel, and arrange around the hummus on the plate. Serve right away.

Cast-Iron Corn Bread

Corn was plentiful in the South, and corn bread was something Addy and Momma ate for breakfast (crumbled in a bowl with buttermilk) or that Momma packed in Addy's lunch pail. This modern version is lightly sweetened with honey and baked in a cast-iron pan. To make corn bread muffins, which are great on the go, divide the batter among greased standard muffin cups and reduce the baking time by a few minutes.

MAKES ONE 10-INCH CORN BREAD

1 cup fine cornmeal

1 cup all-purpose flour, plus flour for dusting

2 teaspoons baking powder

½ teaspoon baking soda

½ teaspoon salt

2 large eggs

1⅓ cups buttermilk

4 tablespoons (½ stick) unsalted butter, melted, plus butter for greasing

¼ cup honey

Preheat the oven to 425°F. Generously butter a 10-inch cast-iron frying pan or square baking pan.

In a medium bowl, whisk together the cornmeal, flour, baking powder, baking soda, and salt. Set aside.

In a large bowl, whisk together the eggs until blended. Add the buttermilk, melted butter, and honey and whisk until blended. Add the cornmeal mixture to the buttermilk mixture and stir until evenly moistened. Scrape the batter into the prepared pan, spreading it evenly, and smooth out the top.

Bake until a toothpick inserted into the center comes out clean, 20 to 25 minutes. Remove the pan from the oven and set it on a wire rack. Let the corn bread cool slightly. Serve warm.

Challah

Traditional Jewish observances like the Sabbath were fundamental in Rebecca's family. Challah (pronounced "haaluh") is a soft, eggy bread traditionally served on the Sabbath, which is a holy day. Although it can be shaped as a round or into rolls and knots, a braided loaf is the most common. Thick slices of leftover or stale challah make exceptional French toast.

MAKES 1 LARGE LOAF

About 5 cups all-purpose flour, plus flour for dusting

¼ cup sugar

1 tablespoon active dry yeast

1 teaspoon salt

1¼ cups lukewarm water (110°F)

6 tablespoons (¾ stick) unsalted butter, at room temperature, plus butter for greasing

3 large eggs

1 tablespoon whole milk

1 tablespoon sesame seeds or poppy seeds (optional)

In a large bowl, using an electric mixer, combine 1½ cups of the flour, the sugar, yeast, and salt. Add the lukewarm water and beat on medium-high speed until well mixed. Beat in the butter and 2 of the eggs. Beat in 3 cups of the flour to make a dough that is semisoft but no longer sticky.

Sprinkle a work surface with flour. Transfer the dough to the floured surface. Knead the dough, adding more flour as needed to prevent sticking, until smooth and elastic, about 5 minutes. Butter a large bowl. Form the dough into a ball, place it in the bowl, and turn the dough to coat all sides. Cover the bowl with a clean kitchen towel and let rise in a warm place until doubled in size, about 1½ hours.

Sprinkle a surface with flour. Turn out the dough onto the floured work surface. Using your hands, press the ball flat and knead until smooth, about 3 minutes. Cut into 3 equal pieces. Cover with a clean kitchen towel to prevent drying. Working with 1 piece at time, using your palms, roll each piece into a rope 20 inches long.

~ *Continued on page 64* ~

Hawaiian Chicken-Pineapple Kebabs with Mango Sauce

Pineapples have long been a symbol of Hawaii, where Nanea lived during World War II, but they are not native to the islands. In fact, they come from South America and were brought to Hawaii in the early 1900s. Fresh pineapple makes a terrific snack on its own but can also be used in many desserts and in savory dishes like this one. Here, chicken and pineapple are threaded onto skewers and grilled, then served with a sweet and tangy mango dipping sauce.

MAKES 6 TO 8 SERVINGS

MANGO DIPPING SAUCE

½ yellow onion, finely chopped

3 tablespoons olive oil

2 mangoes, peeled and finely diced

½ cup fresh orange juice

2 cloves garlic, minced

Juice of 1 lime

2 tablespoons honey

To make the mango dipping sauce, in a small bowl, combine the onion and oil and let soak until the onion has softened, about 10 minutes. Transfer the onion mixture to a nonreactive saucepan. Add the mangoes, orange juice, garlic, lime juice, and honey and stir to mix. Set the pan over medium-high heat and cook, stirring occasionally, until the mango is soft and the flavors are blended, about 15 minutes. Remove from the heat and let cool for 15 minutes.

Transfer the sauce to a blender and purée to the desired consistency. Transfer to a bowl and set aside, or cover and refrigerate until ready to use.

~ *Continued on page 68* ~

~ Continued from page 67 ~

CHICKEN-PINEAPPLE KEBABS

½ cup pineapple juice

3 tablespoons olive oil, plus more for brushing

2 tablespoons reduced-sodium soy sauce

2 tablespoons firmly packed light brown sugar

1 tablespoon minced shallot

1 tablespoon peeled and grated fresh ginger

1 clove garlic, minced

1 pound boneless, skinless chicken breasts, cut into 1-inch cubes

½ pineapple, peeled, cored, and cut into 1-inch cubes

The dipping sauce can be made up to 1 day before serving.

To make the kebabs, in a small bowl, stir together the pineapple juice, oil, soy sauce, brown sugar, shallot, ginger, and garlic. Set the basting sauce aside.

Thread the chicken and pineapple cubes onto 12 to 16 skewers, alternating a chicken cube followed by a pineapple cube, and dividing the chicken and pineapple evenly among the skewers. Brush both the chicken and pineapple lightly with oil, then brush generously with some of the basting sauce.

Place a nonstick stovetop grill pan over medium-high heat and heat for 2 minutes, or prepare a gas or charcoal grill for direct cooking over medium heat (ask an adult for help).

Grill the kebabs, basting them frequently with the remaining basting sauce and turning them with tongs as needed, until the chicken and pineapple are lightly browned on all sides and the chicken is opaque throughout, 7 to 10 minutes. Transfer to a platter.

To serve, divide the mango dipping sauce among small cups or bowls and place alongside the kebabs.

⭐ Meet Nanea Mitchell

Nanea loves the ease and friendliness of her life in Honolulu, Hawaii, in 1941. But when Japan attacks Pearl Harbor, America enters World War II and everything changes. Schools are closed and there are rumors of more attacks. Nanea doesn't let the fact that she's the youngest in her family keep her from helping her community. She makes food for aid workers, performs hula for wounded soldiers, and leads a drive to gather much-needed supplies for the Red Cross. In the spirit of aloha, Nanea proves that no task is too big and no helper is too small.

In Nanea's Kitchen

Hawaii is home to people from many different ethnic backgrounds. The cultural mix is especially evident in the delicious foods found on the islands. In addition to fresh fish and tropical fruit, the cooking traditions from China, Japan, Portugal, the Philippines, and Korea influence Hawaiian meals.

Mochi: A dessert from Japan made with sweet glutinous rice flour and stuffed with a variety of fillings and flavors.
Shave ice: Crushed ice flavored with syrup, also introduced by the Japanese.
Malasada doughnuts: A Portuguese treat of fried yeast dough, typically rolled in granulated sugar and sometimes seasoned with cinnamon.
Portuguese sausage: A sweet and spicy pork sausage from Portugal often served at breakfast.
Crack seed: A Chinese snack of preserved fruit, most often plums.

Luaus

A luau (LOO-ow) is a party or feast with traditional Hawaiian food, music, and entertainment—often hula dancing. Islanders have luaus to celebrate weddings, special birthdays, graduations, and other occasions. Traditionally the food was presented on large woven mats made from ti leaves called lauhalas (LAH-ooh-HAH-lahs), and diners sat on the floor. Popular dishes include:

Kalua pork: Kalua (kah-LOO-ah) means to bake in an underground oven. Kalua pork is salted pork wrapped in banana leaves and cooked in an underground oven or pit called an imu (EE-moo), or three fingers.
Poke: A Japanese-inspired dish that includes chunks of raw fish served over rice.
Laulau: (LAH-ooh LAH-ooh) A dish of fish with chicken, pork, or beef wrapped in ti or taro leaves.
Poi: (POY) A starchy pudding made from mashed taro root.
Lomi: (LOH-mee) A dish of salmon, tomatoes, and onions that is served cold.

Pan-Seared Fish Tacos

These fresh fish tacos would be the perfect meal for Joss and her friends to enjoy on a sunny Southern California beach after a day of surfing. Panfrying instead of deep-frying the spice-rubbed fish makes these tacos simple and keeps them healthy. Any white fish, such as halibut, cod, or sea bass, will work in this recipe.

MAKES 4 SERVINGS

1 tablespoon sweet paprika

1½ teaspoons ground cumin

1 teaspoon garlic powder

1 teaspoon onion powder

1 teaspoon dried oregano

1 teaspoon dried thyme

Salt and ground black pepper

¼ teaspoon cayenne pepper (optional)

1 pound firm white fish, cut into 1½-inch cubes

2 tablespoons olive oil

8 (6-inch) corn tortillas, warmed

FOR SERVING

Shredded cabbage

Sliced avocado

Pico de gallo or salsa

Sour cream

In a small bowl, stir together the paprika, cumin, garlic powder, onion powder, oregano, thyme, 1 teaspoon salt, ½ teaspoon black pepper, and the cayenne pepper (if using). Place the fish in a large bowl, sprinkle with the spice mixture, and toss to coat. Let stand at room temperature for 5 to 10 minutes.

In a large nonstick sauté pan over medium-high heat, warm the oil. Add the fish and cook, stirring occasionally, until just cooked through, about 4 minutes.

To assemble the tacos, fill the center of the tortillas with the fish, then top with cabbage, avocado, pico de gallo, and sour cream.

⭐ Meet Joss Kendrick

Living in sunny Huntington Beach, California, Joss can catch a wave almost any day of the week. When she enters a competition so she can meet her surf idol, there's just one thing standing in her way: the perfect surf video. Her brother Dylan makes the best videos, but the only way he'll film Joss is if she tries out for the cheerleading team. Cheerleading?! No way—Joss is 100 percent surfer girl. And yet . . . it's the only way she's going to meet her surf idol. To do her best in not one but TWO sports, Joss will need to fuel her body with the best foods she can get.

Fuel Up!

Every body needs the vitamins in fruits and veggies. And dairy foods like milk, cheese, and yogurt are loaded with calcium for strong bones.

Carbohydrates store fuel inside muscles—so you want your tank full of them before you train. Some good carbohydrates: whole grain bread, pasta, and cereal; brown rice; potatoes; and peas, beans, and fruit.

Protein gives you energy, helps you grow and recover from exercise, and builds strong muscles. It's actually what muscles are made of! Some good proteins: fish, cheese, chicken, turkey, lean meat, beans, eggs, tofu, milk, and yogurt.

Tips for the Big Day

Eat breakfast! Wake up your body and start the day right with a full tank. If your game or event starts right after school, eating a good lunch is extra important, too.

Don't get greasy. Cheeseburgers and pizza taste great, but they can slow your digestion and make you feel tired. Save them for celebrating!

Time it right. It takes 2 to 3 hours for your body to digest a meal, so it's best not to eat right before you're on. Have a small snack up to 30 minutes before your event.

Healthy Snacks

- Veggies and hummus
- String cheese and an orange
- Trail mix
- Peanut butter crackers
- Granola bars or fig bars
- Low-fat yogurt with fruit

Cookies
& Bars

Mexican Wedding Cookies

These buttery cookies—also known as polvorones or bizcochitos—have a long history, likely making their way to Mexico with Spanish colonists. They are a staple of wedding feasts and holiday parties, like the Christmas celebrations of Josefina's family and village. Chop the almonds by hand or coarsely grind them in a food processor—they should not be as finely ground as almond flour. These cookies are also traditionally made with pecans.

MAKES ABOUT 4 DOZEN COOKIES

1¾ cups all-purpose flour

1 teaspoon ground cinnamon

1 cup (2 sticks) unsalted butter, at room temperature

1½ cups powdered sugar

1 teaspoon vanilla extract

¼ teaspoon salt

1 cup finely chopped toasted almonds or pecans

In a medium bowl, sift together the flour and cinnamon. Set aside.

In a large bowl, using an electric mixer, beat the butter on high speed until fluffy and pale yellow, about 3 minutes. Add ½ cup of the powdered sugar and beat until light and fluffy, about 2 minutes. Turn off the mixer and add the vanilla and salt. Mix on low speed until combined, about 1 minute. Turn off the mixer and scrape down the bowl with a rubber spatula. Add the flour mixture and nuts and beat on low speed just until combined. Cover the bowl with plastic wrap and refrigerate until the dough is chilled but not hard and is no longer sticky to the touch, about 15 minutes.

Preheat the oven to 350°F. Line a cookie sheet with parchment paper.

Scoop up rounded teaspoonfuls of dough and shape the dough into 1-inch balls. Place the balls on the prepared cookie sheet, spacing the cookies about 1 inch apart.

Bake until the cookies are just golden on the bottom, 10 to 12 minutes. Remove the cookie sheet from the oven and set it on a wire rack. Let cool for 5 minutes.

Meanwhile, sift the remaining 1 cup powdered sugar into a shallow bowl. One at a time, roll each cookie in the powdered sugar, place on the rack, and let cool completely.

Ginger Cookies

Chewy gingerbread cakes first became popular during Felicity's time in colonial Williamsburg, and they are still irresistible today. Their ingredients will fill your home with the most delectable spicy aroma. Double the recipe if you like, and keep extra logs of the dough in the freezer for up to 1 month; to bake, thaw a log partially, then slice and bake as directed.

MAKES ABOUT 4 DOZEN COOKIES

2½ cups all-purpose flour

2½ teaspoons baking soda

1½ tablespoons ground ginger

½ teaspoon ground cinnamon

½ teaspoon salt

¼ teaspoon ground white pepper

¾ cup (1½ sticks) plus 2 tablespoons unsalted butter, at room temperature

1¼ cups sugar, plus more for sprinkling

1 large egg

½ cup unsulphured dark molasses

¼ cup minced crystallized ginger

In a medium bowl, sift together the flour, baking soda, ground ginger, cinnamon, salt, and white pepper. Set aside. In a large bowl, using an electric mixer, beat the butter and sugar on medium-high speed until creamy, about 5 minutes. Add the egg and beat until the mixture is fluffy, about 5 minutes. Add the molasses and beat until incorporated. Reduce the speed to low, slowly add the flour mixture, and beat until fully incorporated, 2 to 3 minutes. Stir in the crystallized ginger until evenly distributed.

Lay a sheet of waxed paper on a work surface. Divide the dough in half. Place half of the dough in the center of the waxed paper and form it into a rough log. Fold 1 side of the paper over the dough and press to shape it into an even log about 1½ inches in diameter. Wrap tightly in the waxed paper. Repeat with the remaining dough. Refrigerate the logs until firm, at least 4 hours or up to 2 days.

Preheat the oven to 325°F. Line 2 cookie sheets with parchment paper.

Unwrap the chilled dough and slice into rounds ⅛ inch thick. Arrange the rounds on the prepared cookie sheets, spacing them about 1 inch apart.

Bake until the cookies are golden, 8 to 10 minutes. Remove the cookie sheets from the oven and set them on wire racks. Let cool for 5 minutes, then use a metal spatula to move the cookies directly to the racks. Sprinkle with sugar and let cool completely.

★ Meet Felicity Merriman

Felicity is a girl who loves action and adventure, not the "sitting-down kinds of things" she has to learn to become a proper gentlewoman in 1774 Virginia. Writing with a quill and ink, and any kind of stitchery makes Felicity itch to get outside. Even helping Mother make apple butter on a crisp fall day is too much stirring and standing still. The first chance she gets, Felicity leaves the kitchen to pick apples—by climbing onto the roof!

In Felicity's Kitchen

Without stoves, refrigerators, or running water, the task of cooking took a lot of time. Although Felicity helped her mother in the kitchen, they still needed servants and slaves to prepare meals for the household. Virginians were known for their hospitality, and Felicity's family was always ready to receive friends, family, and travelers—and treat them to a lavish meal.

Popular Foods in Felicity's Time

Coffee: After the Boston Tea Party of 1773, housewives united in a switch to coffee over tea and it became the most common hot drink in households.

Stews and potpies: Pork, beef, and lamb were the center of many meals, whether boiled or served in stews, soups, or potpies. Most families ate meals standing up off of wooden planks called trenchers.

Porridge: Popular for breakfast, mushes and porridges were made from cornmeal, oats, or beans. Corn and beans were staples in most households, and corncakes and corn pone were often served at meals.

Staples: Ingredients such as peanuts, sweet potatoes, collard greens, and rice were brought to the colonies on African slave ships in the 1700s and eventually became staples in the American diet.

Sand Dollar Snickerdoodles

Dusted with cinnamon-sugar and decorated with toasted sliced almonds, these buttery cookies look just like the sandy treasures that Joss and her friends might find when beachcombing along the California coast. Pack them in an airtight container for a seaside picnic, or serve them at home to create a beachy mood no matter how far you live from an ocean.

MAKES ABOUT 3 DOZEN COOKIES

2¾ cups all-purpose flour

1 teaspoon baking powder

1 teaspoon salt

1 cup (2 sticks) unsalted butter, at room temperature

1¾ cups granulated sugar

2 large eggs

2 teaspoons vanilla extract

1 teaspoon ground cinnamon

1 cup sliced almonds

White sanding sugar or turbinado sugar for sprinkling

In a medium bowl, whisk together the flour, baking powder, and salt. Set aside. In a large bowl, using an electric mixer, beat the butter and 1½ cups of the granulated sugar on medium speed until well blended, about 1 minute. Add the eggs one at a time, beating well after each addition. Beat in the vanilla. Reduce the speed to low and gradually beat in the flour mixture just until blended. Turn off the mixer and scrape down the bowl with a rubber spatula. Transfer the dough to the center of a large piece of plastic wrap. Cover the dough with the plastic wrap and shape it into a log about 2 inches in diameter. Refrigerate for at least 30 minutes or up to 1 day.

Preheat the oven to 350°F. Line 2 cookie sheets with parchment paper.

In a small bowl, stir together the remaining ¼ cup granulated sugar and the cinnamon. Spread the cinnamon-sugar on a plate.

Unwrap the chilled dough and roll in the cinnamon-sugar, coating the entire surface. Slice into rounds about ¼ inch thick. Arrange the rounds on the prepared cookie sheets, spacing them about 2 inches apart. In the center of each cookie, arrange 5 almond slices in a circle to create a sand dollar design. Sprinkle the cookies with sanding sugar.

Bake 1 cookie sheet at a time until the cookies are lightly browned at the edges, about 10 minutes. Remove the cookie sheet from the oven and set it on a wire rack. Let cool for 5 minutes, then use a metal spatula to move the cookies. Repeat to bake the rest of the cookies. Let cool completely.

Butterscotch, Coconut & Macadamia Nut Cookies

Macadamia trees are native to Australia. Kira discovers them on her trip to the continent when she spends a summer caring for koalas, kangaroos, and other wildlife. Semisweet, white chocolate, or even peanut butter chips can be swapped for the butterscotch.

MAKES ABOUT 20 COOKIES

1⅓ cups all-purpose flour

½ teaspoon baking powder

½ teaspoon baking soda

½ teaspoon salt

½ cup (1 stick) unsalted butter, at room temperature

½ cup granulated sugar

½ cup firmly packed light brown sugar

1 large egg

½ teaspoon vanilla extract

1¼ cups sweetened shredded coconut

¾ cup macadamia nuts, roughly chopped

½ cup butterscotch chips

Preheat the oven to 325°F. Line a cookie sheet with parchment paper.

In a medium bowl, sift together the flour, baking powder, baking soda, and salt. Set aside.

In a large bowl, using an electric mixer, beat together the butter, granulated sugar, and brown sugar on medium speed until light and fluffy, about 3 minutes. Reduce the speed to low, add the egg and vanilla, and beat until combined, about 1 minute. Turn off the mixer and scrape down the bowl with a rubber spatula. Add the flour mixture and beat on low speed until combined, about 1 minute. Turn off the mixer. Using a rubber spatula, fold in the coconut, macadamia nuts, and butterscotch chips.

Scoop rounded tablespoonfuls of dough onto the prepared cookie sheet, spacing the cookies about 2 inches apart.

Bake until the cookies are golden brown, 16 to 18 minutes. Remove the cookie sheet from the oven and set it on a wire rack. Let cool for 5 minutes, then use a metal spatula to move the cookies directly to the rack. Let cool completely.

★ Meet Kira Bailey

Kira loves animals, so she's thrilled to stay at her aunt's wildlife sanctuary in Australia for the summer. She helps feed and care for the animals, which include kangaroos, koalas, pygmy possums, wombats, and emus. At the wildlife sanctuary, Kira sleeps in a tent, and food is cooked outdoors on a barbecue—even breakfast, or brekkie, as it's often called in Australia. There's nothing like the smell of bacon on the barbecue to wake you up in the morning!

Australian Favorites in Kira's Kitchen

Australia is a multicultural country, and this is reflected in the food, especially in the bigger cities—from curries to pizza, you can find any type of food there. But a whole host of beloved dishes are uniquely Australian.

Meat pies: Even though fillings may vary, the most common meat pies are made with diced or minced meat and gravy and often onions, mushrooms, and cheese or potatoes. They are frequently eaten with ketchup.

Vegemite: This thick, dark brown spread is made from leftover brewers' yeast extract and spices and is often served served on toast, crumpets, or crackers. It's a childhood favorite.

Barbecue: Grilling in Australia is a much-loved, year-round pastime, where sausages, prawns, lamb chops, and steaks are sizzled on the "barbie."

Pavlova: In this iconic Australian dessert, a crunchy-chewy meringue base holds clouds of whipped cream and tart-sweet fruits like kiwi, strawberries, mango, or berries.

Lamingtons: Probably the most-loved cake of Australia! Tender vanilla sponge cake is dipped in chocolate sauce, then coated in finely chopped coconut. Sometimes the cakes are sandwiched with cream and raspberry jam.

Damper bread: This traditional soda bread is cooked in hot ashes and dipped in golden syrup. It's called "damper" bread because it was said to "dampen" the fire by early settlers in Australia.

Sugar-&-Spice Star Sandwich Cookies

A layer of sweet berry jam binds these spiced molasses sandwich cookies. Luciana would like star shapes as she dreams of traveling to outer space, but you can use any shaped cutters you like, such as rounds or hearts. Whatever their shape, these cookies are out of this world!

MAKES ABOUT 2 DOZEN SANDWICH COOKIES

2¾ cups all-purpose flour

1 teaspoon baking powder

1 teaspoon
ground cinnamon

1 teaspoon
ground allspice

¼ teaspoon
ground nutmeg

¼ teaspoon baking soda

¼ teaspoon salt

¾ cup (1½ sticks)
plus 2 tablespoons
unsalted butter, at
room temperature

1 cup firmly packed
dark brown sugar

1 large egg

1 tablespoon unsulphured
dark molasses

1 tablespoon heavy cream

1 cup strawberry or
raspberry jam

Powdered sugar,
for dusting

In a medium bowl, whisk together the flour, baking powder, baking soda, cinnamon, allspice, nutmeg, and salt. Set aside. In a large bowl, using an electric mixer, beat the butter and brown sugar on medium-high speed until light and fluffy, 2 to 3 minutes. Reduce the speed to low, add the egg and molasses, and beat until well combined. Add the flour mixture and and beat just until blended. Add the cream and beat just until combined. Form the dough into a disk, wrap it tightly in plastic wrap, and refrigerate until firm, at least 1 hour or up to overnight.

Preheat the oven to 350°F. Line 2 cookie sheets with parchment paper.

Sprinkle a work surface with flour. Dump the dough onto the floured surface. Roll out the dough about ¼ inch thick. Using a 3-inch star-shaped cookie cutter, cut out as many cookies as possible. Transfer the cookies to the prepared cookie sheets, spacing them about 1 inch apart. Gather up the dough scraps, press them together, roll them out again, and cut out more cookies. Use a smaller star-shaped cookie cutter to cut out the center from half of the larger stars, then remove the dough from the centers.

Bake 1 cookie sheet at a time until the tips of the cookies are golden brown, 10 to 12 minutes. Remove the cookie sheet from the oven and set it on a wire rack. Let cool for 5 minutes, then use a metal spatula to move the cookies directly to the rack. Repeat to bake to bake the rest of the cookies. Let cool completely.

Using a small icing spatula, spread a layer of jam on the flat side of each solid cookie Top with the cut-out cookies, dust lightly with powdered sugar, and serve.

Cowboy Cookies

Made with oats, chocolate chips, toasted pecans, and shredded coconut, these hearty cookies were so popular in the 1950s that they were taught in home economics classes. These cookies were Maryellen's favorite treat to snack on when she watched Westerns on TV. For classic oatmeal–chocolate chip cookies, leave out the pecans and coconut.

MAKES ABOUT 2 DOZEN COOKIES

1½ cups all-purpose flour

2 teaspoons baking powder

1 teaspoon baking soda

**1 teaspoon
ground cinnamon**

¼ teaspoon salt

**¾ cup (1½ sticks)
unsalted butter,
at room temperature**

¾ cup granulated sugar

**¾ cup firmly packed
dark brown sugar**

2 large eggs

2 teaspoons vanilla extract

2 cups rolled oats

**1 cup semisweet
chocolate chips**

**¾ cup shredded
unsweetened coconut, plus
more for sprinkling**

**½ cup chopped toasted
pecans or walnuts**

 Preheat the oven to 350°F. Line a cookie sheet with parchment paper.

In a medium bowl, sift together the flour, baking powder, baking soda, cinnamon, and salt. Set aside.

In a large bowl, using an electric mixer, beat the butter, granulated sugar, and brown sugar on medium speed until light and fluffy, about 3 minutes. Reduce the speed to low and add the eggs one at a time, beating well after each addition. Add the vanilla and beat until combined, about 1 minute. Turn off the mixer and scrape down the bowl with a rubber spatula. Add the flour mixture and beat on low speed until combined, about 1 minute. Turn off the mixer and stir in the oats, chocolate chips, coconut, and nuts.

Scoop rounded tablespoonfuls of dough onto the prepared cookie sheet, spacing the cookies about 3 inches apart. Sprinkle shredded coconut on top of each cookie.

Bake until the cookies are golden brown, 15 to 17 minutes. Remove the cookie sheet from the rack. Using a metal spatula, move the cookies to a wire rack and let cool completely.

Spiced Molasses Flower Cookies

Melody loved arranging flowers. She learned everything from her grandfather, who had a flower shop in Detroit. These fun flower cookies don't smell like the flowers Melody grows in her garden but will fill the house with the delicious aroma of molasses and spices.

MAKES ABOUT 18 COOKIES

SPICED MOLASSES COOKIES

2½ cups all-purpose flour, plus flour for dusting

2 teaspoons ground ginger

½ teaspoon ground cinnamon

½ teaspoon baking soda

½ teaspoon salt

¼ teaspoon ground nutmeg

½ cup (1 stick) unsalted butter, at room temperature

¼ cup granulated sugar

¼ cup firmly packed light brown sugar

1 large egg

½ cup unsulphured dark molasses

To make the cookies, in a medium bowl, whisk together the flour, ginger, cinnamon, baking soda, salt, and nutmeg. Set aside.

In a large bowl, using an electric mixer, beat together the butter, granulated sugar, and brown sugar on medium speed until light and fluffy, about 2 minutes. Add the egg and beat until blended, about 1 minute. Reduce the speed to low and gradually beat in the molasses until blended. Turn off the mixer and scrape down the bowl with a rubber spatula. Add the flour mixture and beat on low speed until combined, about 30 seconds.

Sprinkle a work surface with flour. Dump the dough onto the floured surface and press it into a mound. Divide the dough in half and shape each half into a thick disk. Wrap each disk in plastic wrap and refrigerate for at least 1 hour or up to 2 days.

Line 2 cookie sheets with parchment paper. Sprinkle a work surface with flour. Place 1 dough disk on the floured surface. Roll out the dough into a round ¼ inch thick. Using a 4-inch flower-shaped cookie cutter, cut out as many cookies as possible. Use a metal spatula to transfer the cookies to a prepared cookie sheet, spacing them at least 1 inch apart. Gather up the dough scraps, press them together, wrap in plastic wrap, and refrigerate.

~ *Continued on page 90* ~

~ *Continued from page 89* ~

LEMON ICING

1½ cups powdered sugar

3 tablespoons fresh lemon juice, plus more if needed

A few drops yellow and green gel food coloring (optional)

White nonpareils, for decorating (optional)

Repeat with the second chilled dough disk. Then combine the dough scraps from both disks, press them into a disk, roll out, and cut out more flowers. If the dough becomes too warm to work with, wrap and refrigerate for 10 minutes before rerolling. Refrigerate the cutout cookies while you preheat the oven.

Position 2 racks in the oven so that they are evenly spaced and preheat the oven to 375°F.

Bake the cookies, rotating the cookie sheets between the racks halfway through baking, until lightly browned on the bottom, 8 to 10 minutes. Remove the cookie sheets from the oven and set them on wire racks. Let cool for 5 minutes, then use a metal spatula to move the cookies directly to the racks. Let cool completely.

To make the icing, sift the powdered sugar into a bowl, then whisk in the lemon juice until completely smooth. Add a few drops of food coloring (if using). Add more lemon juice to the icing if needed to create a thick but spreadable consistency.

Using a small offset or icing spatula, spread the yellow icing in a thin layer over the top of each cookie. Sprinkle a pinch of nonpareils (if using) onto the center of each cookie while the icing is still wet, then let stand until the icing is set, about 20 minutes, before serving.

⭐ Meet Melody Ellison

Melody loves to sing. She's growing up in the 1960s listening to the music that made Detroit famous: Motown. She's also listening to the talk around the dinner table. It's about justice and equality and standing up to discrimination. Inspired by the words of Dr. Martin Luther King, Jr., Melody finds a way to use her own voice to speak up about fairness.

In Melody's Kitchen

Melody's favorite part of the week is having dinner at her grandparents' house after church every Sunday. Inspired by their Southern roots, the family would enjoy pot roast or fried chicken, corn bread and dressing, fresh vegetables, grits, peach cobbler, and sweet potato pie. Melody inherited a love of gardening from her grandfather, and she grew tomatoes, green beans, corn, and carrots in her own backyard. Melody's vegetables were often part of Sunday dinner.

Sharing a Meal

Melody and her family often had a meal with their church family. Everyone would bring a dish to pass as they gathered in the church basement for food and fellowship. Block parties and backyard barbecues were also popular. Neighbors enjoyed grilled hamburgers and hot dogs, home-grown fruits and veggies, fresh-squeezed lemonade, and plenty of homemade baked goods.

Detroit Classics

Everyone in Detroit knew what a "Coney Island" was: a hot dog with chili, onion, and mustard. Another local favorite, the "Boston Cooler," was Vernors ginger ale with vanilla ice cream.

Mexican Hot Chocolate Cookies

Cacao plants are native to the region that is now present-day Mexico. Here, the flavors of Mexican hot chocolate, with a hint of cinnamon and zingy chile powder, are transformed into delicious cookies. The marshmallows are a fun surprise on top.

MAKES ABOUT 26 COOKIES

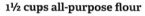

1½ cups all-purpose flour

½ cup unsweetened cocoa powder

½ cup hot chocolate mix

1 teaspoon baking powder

1 teaspoon ancho chile pepper

½ teaspoon ground cinnamon, plus more for dusting

¼ teaspoon salt

3 large eggs

1⅔ cups sugar

2 teaspoons vanilla extract

4 tablespoons (½ stick) unsalted butter, melted and cooled slightly

1 bag mini marshmallows or 13 regular-size marshmallows, halved crosswise

 In a medium bowl, whisk together the flour, cocoa powder, hot chocolate mix, baking powder, ancho chile, cinnamon, and salt. Set aside.

In a large bowl, using an electric mixer, beat the eggs, sugar, and vanilla on high speed until light in color and thick, about 3 minutes. Add the melted butter and beat on medium speed until blended. Turn off the mixer and scrape down the bowl with a rubber spatula. Add the flour mixture and beat on low speed just until blended. Cover the bowl with plastic wrap and refrigerate for 1 hour.

Position 2 racks so that they are evenly spaced in the oven and preheat the oven to 350°F. Line 2 cookie sheets with parchment paper. Scoop up heaping tablespoonfuls of the chilled dough, roll them into balls between the palms of your hands, and place on the prepared cookie sheets, spacing them 2 inches apart.

Bake until the cookies are puffed and dry, 10 to 12 minutes, rotating the cookie sheets between the racks, halfway through baking. Let cool on wire racks for 5 minutes, then move the cookies directly to the racks.

Arrange the cookies in a single layer on one unlined cookie sheet. Position an oven rack 6 inches below the broiler and preheat the broiler. Place a few mini marshmallows in the center of each cookie (if using regular size, place a marshmallow half, cut-side down, in the center of each cookie). Broil until the marshmallows are gooey and golden (watch them carefully!). Let cool on a wire rack. Just before serving, put a spoonful of cinnamon in a fine-mesh sieve and lightly dust the cookies with a little cinnamon.

Chocolate-Vanilla Sandwich Cookies

The original "Oreo biscuit" was invented in New York City in the early 1900s, around the time Rebecca lived there. They have remained the best-selling cookie in the United States for more than a century.

MAKES ABOUT 1 DOZEN SANDWICH COOKIES

COOKIES

1¼ cups all-purpose flour, plus flour for dusting

¾ cup granulated sugar

¾ cup unsweetened Dutch-process cocoa powder

1 teaspoon baking soda

¼ teaspoon baking powder

¼ teaspoon salt

¾ cup (1½ sticks) unsalted butter, at room temperature

1 large egg plus 1 large egg yolk

FILLING

½ cup (1 stick) unsalted butter, at room temperature

1½ cups powdered sugar

1 tablespoon whole milk

1 teaspoon vanilla extract

To make the cookies, preheat the oven to 375°F. Line a cookie sheet with parchment paper.

In a large bowl, whisk together the flour, granulated sugar, cocoa powder, baking soda, baking powder, and salt. Add the butter. Using an electric mixer, beat until incorporated, about 2 minutes. Add the egg and egg yolk and beat on low speed until blended. Raise the speed to medium and beat until the dough comes together, about 2 minutes.

Sprinkle a work surface with flour. Dump the dough onto the floured surface. Roll out the dough about ¼ inch thick. Using a 2-inch round cutter, cut out as many cookies as possible. Transfer the cookies to the prepared cookie sheet, spacing them about 2 inches apart. Gather up the dough scraps, press them together, roll them out again, and cut out more cookies, refrigerating the dough for 15 minutes if it gets too warm.

Bake until the cookies are firm to the touch, 8 to 10 minutes. Remove the cookie sheet from the oven and set it on a wire rack. Let cool for 5 minutes, then use a metal spatula to move the cookies directly to the rack. Let cool completely.

Meanwhile, make the filling: In a large bowl, using an electric mixer, beat together the butter, powdered sugar, milk, and vanilla on medium-high speed until smooth and well combined, about 3 minutes. Fit a piping bag with a ½-inch tip. Spoon the filling into the bag, then pipe a layer of the filling (about 2 teaspoons) on the flat side of half of the cookies. Top with the remaining cookies, flat side down, and gently press together.

★ Meet Rebecca Rubin

In Rebecca's bustling 1914 New York City neighborhood, the streets are filled with the sounds of many languages and the smells of foods from around the world. Her family are Russian-Jewish immigrants, and Rebecca loves the traditions and holidays they brought with them from the Old Country, like serving tea from a samovar and lighting candles on Hanukkah. But Rebecca wants to do American things, too, like see a motion picture—and maybe even act in one!

In Rebecca's Kitchen

When Rebecca arrives home from school and enters her small apartment, she's greeted by the delicious aroma of her mother's challah. Rebecca opens the oven and knocks on a loaf to see if the challah is done baking—it will make a hollow sound if it's ready! The holidays bring the sound and smell of fried potato pancakes sizzling in oil. Rebecca peels

lots of potatoes so that there are enough latkes for everyone in her large family! On hot summer days, she and her cousin Ana squeeze lemons and add sugar and water. Then Rebecca opens the icebox and breaks off a chip of ice to chill their lemonade.

Dishes that Rebecca's family would have eaten in the early 1900s

- Noodle kugel, or casserole
- Cheese blintzes
- Chicken and matzo ball soup
- Rugelach pastry
- Pickled herring

Caramel Squares

With layers of buttery shortbread, smooth caramel, and rich chocolate, caramel squares are a yummy treat found in nearly every Australian bakery. Many versions Down Under add toasted coconut to the shortbread. Caramel squares are even better when they are homemade, and of course, when shared between friends like Kira and Alexis.

MAKES 20 SQUARES

SHORTBREAD CRUST

1 cup all-purpose flour

¼ cup firmly packed dark brown sugar

2½ teaspoons cornstarch

¼ teaspoon salt

½ cup (1 stick) cold unsalted butter, cut into cubes, plus butter for greasing

2 tablespoons cold water

1 large egg yolk

Preheat the oven to 350°F. Line a 9-inch baking dish with aluminum foil, pushing it into the corners and letting the foil overhang by about 2 inches on 2 opposite sides. Repeat with the other sides of the dish. Butter the foil.

To make the crust, in a food processor, combine the flour, brown sugar, cornstarch, and salt and pulse until blended. Add the butter and process until the mixture resembles coarse sand. Add the cold water and egg yolk and process until moist clumps form and the dough just begins to come together.

Transfer the dough to the prepared pan and press evenly into the bottom of the pan. Pierce the dough all over with a fork and bake until golden brown, about 20 minutes. Remove the pan from the oven and set it on a wire rack (ask an adult for help if needed). Let cool slightly.

~ *Continued on page 98* ~

~ *Continued from page 97* ~

CARAMEL

1 (14-ounce) can sweetened condensed milk

½ cup plus 2 tablespoons firmly packed dark brown sugar

7 tablespoons unsalted butter, cut into pieces

2 tablespoons light corn syrup

1½ teaspoons vanilla extract

¼ teaspoon salt

CHOCOLATE TOPPING

1½ cups semisweet chocolate chips

¼ cup heavy cream

Sea salt, for sprinkling (optional)

To make the caramel, in a medium saucepan, whisk together the condensed milk and brown sugar. Add the butter, corn syrup, vanilla, .and salt and whisk until combined.. Set the pan over medium heat and bring to a gentle boil. Cook, whisking constantly, until the mixture has darkened slightly, is thickened, and registers 220°F on a candy thermometer, 7 to 10 minutes. If the caramel begins to scorch, reduce the heat. Remove the pan from the heat and carefully pour the caramel over the warm crust. Let cool until the caramel is set, about 20 minutes.

To make the chocolate topping, in a microwave-safe bowl, combine the chocolate chips and cream. Microwave on high in 30-second intervals, stirring in between, until the chocolate is almost completely melted, then stir until smooth. Pour the chocolate over the set caramel, spread in an even layer, and let cool slightly. Sprinkle sea salt (if using) over the chocolate.

Cover the dish with plastic wrap and refrigerate until firm, at least 2 hours or up to overnight. Holding the ends of the foil, lift the dessert onto a cutting board and cut into squares.

Mini Coconut-Lemon Bars

It's hard to picture Hawaii without envisioning tall coconut palm trees swaying in the breeze along sandy beaches. And because of its tropical climate and lush soil, coconut trees have thrived in Hawaii, even though they are not native to the islands that Nanea called home. Adding shredded coconut to the creamy lemon-curd filling gives these bars tropical twist.

MAKES 48 BARS

CRUST

1½ cups all-purpose flour

½ cup powdered sugar

1½ teaspoons finely grated lemon zest

⅛ teaspoon salt

¾ cup (1½ sticks) cold unsalted butter, cut into ½-inch pieces

COCONUT-LEMON FILLING

6 large eggs

2½ cups granulated sugar

¾ cup fresh lemon juice

1 tablespoon finely grated lemon zest

2 cups sweetened shredded coconut

½ cup all-purpose flour

Preheat the oven to 325°F. Line a 9-by-13-inch baking pan with parchment paper, letting the paper overhang on 2 opposite sides of the pan.

To make the crust, in a large bowl, stir together the flour, powdered sugar, lemon zest, and salt. Using a pastry blender or 2 butter knives, cut in the butter just until the mixture forms large, coarse crumbs the size of small peas. Firmly and evenly press the dough into the bottom and 1 inch up the sides of the prepared pan. Bake just until the edges are lightly browned, about 20 minutes. Remove the pan from the oven and set it on a wire rack. Let cool.

Reduce the oven temperature to 300°F.

To make the filling, in a large bowl, whisk the eggs just until blended. Add the granulated sugar and lemon zest and juice and whisk until smooth, about 1 minute. Add the coconut and mix well. Sift the flour into the bowl and whisk until incorporated Slowly pour the filling into the crust. Bake until the filling looks set and does not wobble when the pan is shaken, 40 to 45 minutes. .

Remove the pan from the oven and set it on a wire rack. Let cool to room temperature, about 1 hour. Cover the pan with plastic wrap and refrigerate until firm, at least 4 hours.

Holding the ends of the parchment, lift the dessert onto a cutting board and cut into rectangles.

Mocha Chocolate Brownies

You'd never know that these decadent chocolate brownies topped with a coffee-infused layer are vegan, but they are! Perfect for anyone, like Blaire, who is lactose intolerant but still loves to bake. Make sure not to overbake the brownies, they should look slightly underbaked in the middle so they stay moist and fudgy.

MAKES 9 BROWNIES

BROWNIES

1½ cups all-purpose flour

¾ cup unsweetened cocoa powder

¾ cup granulated sugar

2 tablespoons cornstarch or arrowroot

1 teaspoon baking powder

½ teaspoon salt

½ cup maple syrup

½ cup coconut milk

½ cup coconut oil, melted

1 ounce unsweetened dark chocolate, melted

1 tablespoon vanilla extract

MOCHA LAYER

¼ cup coconut milk

2 tablespoons instant coffee

¼ cup coconut oil, melted

1 cup powdered sugar, sifted

Preheat the oven to 350°F. Line a 9-inch square baking pan with parchment paper.

To make the brownies, in a large bowl, whisk together the flour, cocoa powder, granulated sugar, arrowroot, baking powder, and salt. In a medium bowl, stir together the maple syrup, coconut milk, coconut oil, melted chocolate, and vanilla. Stir the maple syrup mixture into the flour mixture just until mixed. Spoon the batter into the prepared pan and smooth the top.

Bake until the top looks cracked and dry, about 30 minutes. The middle should be slightly underbaked. Remove the pan from the oven and set it on a wire rack. Let cool. Refrigerate the cooled brownies until completely chilled.

Meanwhile, make the mocha layer: In a medium bowl, stir together the coconut milk and instant coffee until the coffee granules are dissolved. Stir in the coconut oil until smooth, then stir in the powdered sugar. The mixture should be easily spreadable.

Using an offset spatula, spread the mocha layer evenly over the cold brownies. Refrigerate for at least 1 hour, or tightly covered for up to 1 week. Cut into squares to serve.

Seashell Madeleines

Joss and her best friend, Sofia, were ready to prove that girls are every bit as strong, skilled, and committed to surfing as boys, so they spent a lot of time at the beach, catching the biggest waves. Cakelike madeleines are baked in shell-shaped molds and then dipped in a sea of white chocolate, so they look an awful lot like the pretty shells you might find on any beach.

MAKES 1 DOZEN MADELEINES

2 large eggs

⅓ cup sugar

¼ teaspoon salt

1 teaspoon vanilla extract

½ cup all-purpose flour, plus flour for dusting

4 tablespoons (½ stick) unsalted butter, melted and cooled, plus melted butter for greasing

⅓ cup white chocolate chips

Preheat the oven to 375°F. Using a pastry brush, coat the 12 molds of a madeleine pan with melted butter, making sure to coat every ridge and flute. Dust the molds with flour, tilting and shaking the pan to coat the surfaces evenly, then tap out any excess.

In a large bowl, using an electric mixer, beat the eggs, sugar, and salt on medium-high speed until light and fluffy, about 5 minutes. Add the vanilla and beat until blended. Turn off the mixer and scrape down the bowl with a rubber spatula. Sift the flour over the egg mixture. Beat on low speed just until the flour is incorporated. Turn off the mixer. Using a rubber spatula, gently fold in half of the melted butter just until blended. Then gently fold in the remaining melted butter. Scoop a heaping tablespoon of the batter into each prepared mold.

Bake the madeleines until the tops spring back when lightly touched, 10 to 12 minutes. Remove the pan from the oven. Invert the pan onto a wire rack and tap the pan on the rack to release the madeleines. If any of them stick, use a butter knife to loosen the edges, then invert and tap again. Let cool completely.

Line a cookie sheet with parchment paper. Put the chocolate chips in a small microwave-safe bowl. Microwave on high for 20 seconds, stir, then microwave in 15-second intervals, stirring in between just until the chocolate is melted and smooth. Do not overheat the chocolate or it will seize (become thick and lumpy). One at a time, dip the wide, rounded end of each madeleine into the chocolate, then set the madeleine, fluted side up, on the prepared cookie sheet.

Refrigerate the madeleines until the chocolate is set, 10 to 15 minutes, then serve. They are best eaten the same day they are baked.

Nut, Seed & Fruit Granola Bars

The Nez Percé traveled with the seasons to gather food, hunt, and fish.
Kaya often carried fresh or dried berries with her to eat if she got hungry.
These chewy bars are a healthy on-the-go snack, perfect for traveling,
and packed with seeds, nut butter, and dried fruits. You can swap out the
dried apricots with dried cranberries or raisins.

MAKES 12 TO 16 BARS

Nonstick cooking spray

2½ cups old-fashioned rolled oats

1½ cups finely chopped dried apricots

½ cup toasted sunflower seeds

½ cup wheat germ

1 teaspoon ground cinnamon

½ teaspoon salt

½ cup (1 stick) unsalted butter, cut into pieces

½ cup firmly packed light brown sugar

½ cup creamy almond or peanut butter

⅓ cup maple syrup

2 large egg whites

 Preheat the oven to 350°F. Spray a 9-by-13-inch baking pan with nonstick cooking spray.

In a large bowl, combine the oats, apricots, sunflower seeds, wheat germ, cinnamon, and salt and stir with a rubber spatula. Set aside. In a small saucepan, combine the butter, brown sugar, almond butter, and maple syrup. Set the pan over medium heat, bring to a simmer, and cook for 1 minute, stirring constantly with the spatula. Remove from the heat and pour over the oat mixture. Stir with the spatula to mix well. Let cool for 5 minutes.

In a small bowl, whisk the egg whites until frothy, about 30 seconds. Add the egg whites to the oat mixture and stir to combine.

Pour the mixture into the prepared pan. Using the spatula, press the mixture firmly to create an even layer.

Bake until the edges are golden brown and the top is no longer sticky to the touch, 20 to 25 minutes. Remove the pan from the oven and set it on a wire rack. Let cool slightly. Cut into 12 rectangular or 16 square bars, then let cool completely in the pan for 1 hour.

Cakes
& Pies

Pink Velvet Cupcakes with Strawberries

This playful version of red velvet cake gets a blast of fresh flavor from freeze-dried strawberries. Adding the berries to the buttermilk cake batter and the cream cheese frosting makes the cakes pretty and pink, Kirsten's favorite color. Decorate with pink or white sprinkles or top each cupcake with a fresh strawberry right before serving.

MAKES 20 CUPCAKES

PINK VELVET CUPCAKES

2 tablespoons unsweetened cocoa powder, sifted

⅓ cup boiling water

1 cup buttermilk

1 cup freeze-dried strawberries

2 cups all-purpose flour

¼ teaspoon salt

¾ cup (1½ sticks) unsalted butter, at room temperature

1½ cups granulated sugar

3 large eggs

2 teaspoons vanilla extract

Pink gel food coloring

1½ teaspoons baking soda

1 teaspoon white vinegar

Preheat the oven to 350°F. Line 20 cups of two standard 12-cup muffin pans with paper or foil liners.

To make the cupcakes, in a medium heatproof bowl, whisk together the cocoa powder and boiling water until well combined, then whisk in the buttermilk. Set aside.

Place the freeze-dried strawberries in a heavy-duty zippered plastic bag and seal the bag. Using a rolling pin or wooden spoon, crush the strawberries to a fine powder. In a small bowl, whisk together the flour, salt, and strawberry powder.

In a large bowl, using an electric mixer, beat the butter and granulated sugar on medium speed until light and fluffy, 2 to 3 minutes. Add the eggs one at a time, beating well after each addition. Add the vanilla and 3 drops of pink food coloring and beat until combined. Reduce the speed to low, add about half of the flour mixture, and beat just until blended. Pour in the cocoa-buttermilk mixture and beat until combined. Add the remaining flour mixture and beat just until blended. In a small bowl, stir together the baking soda and vinegar, then quickly add the mixture to the batter and stir with a rubber spatula until combined. Divide the batter evenly among the prepared muffin cups.

~ *Continued on page 110* ~

~ *Continued from page 109* ~

STRAWBERRY–CREAM CHEESE FROSTING

½ cup freeze-dried strawberries

2 (8-ounce) packages cream cheese, at room temperature

¾ cup (1½ sticks) unsalted butter, at room temperature

2 teaspoons vanilla extract

2 cups powdered sugar, sifted

Red, pink, and heart-shaped sprinkles, for decorating (optional)

Bake until a wooden skewer inserted into the center of a cupcake comes out clean, about 18 minutes. Remove the pans from the oven and set them on a wire rack. Let cool for 10 minutes, then carefully transfer the cupcakes directly to the rack. Let cool completely, about 1 hour.

To make the frosting, place the freeze-dried strawberries in the zippered plastic bag and seal the bag. Using a rolling pin or a wooden spoon, crush the strawberries to a fine powder. In a large bowl, using an electric mixer, beat the cream cheese, butter, and vanilla on medium-high speed until light and fluffy, about 2 minutes. Turn off the mixer and scrape down the bowl with a rubber spatula. Add about half of the powdered sugar and beat on low speed until well blended. Turn off the mixer, add the remaining sugar and the strawberry powder, and beat on medium speed until smooth. The frosting should be spreadable; if it is too soft, cover the bowl and refrigerate it for about 15 minutes.

Using a pastry bag fitted with a star tip, frost the cupcakes, then decorate them with sprinkles (if using).

★ Meet Kirsten Larson

Kirsten and her family arrive in America in 1854, after a long sea voyage. Eveything looks so different from the life Kirsten knew back in Sweden—the ways people talk and dress seem strange! When the Larsons finally reach a tiny farm on the edge of the frontier, Kirsten believes Papa's promise—America is a land filled with opportunity. And when she discovers that life in America has room for the treasures and traditions from Sweden, Kirsten finally feels at home.

In Kirsten's Kitchen

Making meals was the biggest job girls and women had on the frontier in the 1850s. In the Larson's one-room log cabin, the kitchen was also the dining room, living room, and bedroom. The cabin didn't have electricity or running water, and there was no refrigerator, microwave, or dishwasher to make the work easier. Several times a day, Kirsten walked to the creek and hauled buckets of water back to the cabin for drinking, cooking, and washing dishes.

There were no supermarkets on the frontier. Towns had a general store where farmers bought flour, sugar, salt, rice, and other staples. But the closest town could be miles away, and most families only made the trip a few times a year. Pioneers ate what they could grow or gather. They got milk, butter, and cheese from their cows or goats; gathered eggs from their chickens; and foraged for apples, nuts, and berries in the woods. Meat was raised, hunted,

or trapped. Pioneers built root cellars to keep produce cool and dry so it would last during the winter without freezing.

Foods in Kirsten's Time

These foods reminded Kirsten of Sweden, and especially of the family and friends she loved.

Skansk grot: (SKONE-sk groot) This Swedish porridge is made with rice, apples, and raisins. It was often enjoyed for dessert, and leftovers were kept warm in the oven overnight for a special breakfast treat.

Potato soup: In many Swedish homes, potatoes were part of every meal.

Swedish meatballs: Made with ground pork and ground beef or venison, this dish is hearty and filling.

Swedish pancakes: After a supper of pea soup, these thin pancakes were often served for dessert.

Pepparkakor cookies: These thin, spicy cookies are rolled and cut into festive holiday shapes.

St. Lucia buns: To mark the beginning of the holiday season. the buns are served just before dawn on St. Lucia Day.

Dulce de Leche Crepe Cake

Dulce de leche is a thick, sweet caramel from Latin America made by slowly cooking sweetened milk. It was introduced by Spanish colonists, who for hundreds of years ruled over a vast territory of the Americas, including the newly independent nation of Mexico, where Josefina and her family lived. Today, dulce de leche flavors all types of desserts, from cakes and cookies to tarts and ice cream. Here, delicate crepes are layered with dulce de leche whipped cream for a decadent dessert.

MAKES 8 TO 10 SERVINGS

CREPES

9 large eggs

1½ cups whole milk

1½ cups all-purpose flour

¼ cup plus 1 tablespoon powdered sugar

1 tablespoon vanilla extract

1 teaspoon salt

DULCE DE LECHE WHIPPED CREAM

1 cup plus 2 tablespoons granulated sugar

6 tablespoons (¾ stick) cold unsalted butter, cut into small pieces

¼ teaspoon salt

1½ cups evaporated milk

3 cups heavy cream

To make the crepes, in a blender, combine the eggs, milk, flour, powdered sugar, vanilla, and salt and blend until well combined, about 45 seconds. Stop the blender and scrape down the sides of the bowl, then blend for 30 seconds longer.

Line a rimmed baking sheet with parchment paper. Heat a 10-inch crepe pan or nonstick frying pan over medium-low heat (do not grease the pan). Ladle about ¼ cup of the batter into the center of the pan, then quickly lift and rotate the pan to spread the batter to the edges. If the batter begins to set before spreading, reduce the heat. Cook until the crepe is almost completely cooked through, about 2 minutes. Using a rubber spatula and your fingers, carefully flip the crepe over and cook for 15 seconds longer. Transfer the crepe to the prepared baking sheet to cool. Repeat with the remaining batter, stacking the crepes on top of each other. Let the crepes cool completely before assembling the cake.

To make the dulce de leche, prepare an ice water bath in a large bowl. Put the granulated sugar in a large saucepan. Set the pan over medium-high heat and stir until the sugar begins to melt. Continue stirring, breaking up clumps of sugar as they form, until all of the sugar has melted and turned

~ *Continued on page 114* ~

~ *Continued from page 113* ~

a golden caramel color, 8 to 10 minutes. Add the butter (the mixture will start to bubble) and salt and stir until the butter has melted. While stirring constantly, slowly stir in the evaporated milk (the mixture will continue to bubble) and cook, stirring occasionally, until the mixture is bubbling toward the top of the pan and has formed a cohesive caramel-like texture, about 5 minutes. Remove from the heat and place the saucepan in the ice bath. Stir until the dulce de leche is cool to the touch, then remove the pan from the ice bath and let stand at room temperature to cool completely.

In a large bowl, using an electric mixer, beat the cream on medium-high speed until soft peaks form, about 3 minutes. Using a rubber spatula, fold in half of the dulce de leche until fully incorporated. Reserve the remaining dulce de leche for drizzling over the cake.

To assemble the cake, place 1 crepe on a cake stand or serving plate. Top with a generous dollop of the dulce de leche whipped cream and spread evenly over the crepe. Repeat with the remaining crepes and whipped cream, finishing with a crepe. Refrigerate until ready to serve.

Just before serving, heat the remaining dulce de leche over low heat until slightly loosened but not hot. Pour over the cake and let drizzle down the sides. Cut the cake into wedges and serve.

★ Meet Josefina Montoya

In 1824, Josefina and her sisters work together to help their Santa Fe rancho run smoothly. Out in the courtyard, they husk corn and string chiles to dry just as their Mamá had taught them before she died. In the kitchen, the girls make Papá's favorites: tamales, spicy stews, and sweet bizcochito cookies. The kitchen had a bed above the fireplace, where Josefina tended a sick baby goat that became her pet and followed her everywhere! She named the goat Sombrita, the Spanish word for "shadow."

Healing Foods

Josefina hoped to be a curandera, or healer, one day, just like her Tía Magdalena. When illness struck, each rancho had a store of home remedies to try. When those didn't work, villagers went to the curandera, who was skilled in making medicines.

Chiles contain a chemical that heats without burning the skin and stops pain without killing nerves. Medicines made from chiles eased pain, helped heal wounds, and cured frostbite.

Curenderas used mint leaves to ease stomachaches, ground pumpkin stems to soothe sore throats, and a plant called inmortal to make a person sneeze and sneeze a cold away!

Pueblo Indians

By the time Josefina was a girl, Pueblo Indians and Spanish settlers had been living as neighbors for many years. The Pueblo people were one of several Indian communities that built villages out of adobe clay, crafted beautiful pottery, and farmed.

Pueblo Indians were mostly vegetarian. They had 40 different ways of cooking corn! Pueblo women ground dried corn kernels on a rough stone and moved to smoother stones to grind the corn finer.

Pueblo Indians also raised turkeys and chickens for food. They prized parrots from Mexico for their brilliantly colored feathers and used them to adorn their clothing.

Red, White & Blueberry Sheet Cake

This patriotic buttermilk cake is topped with fluffy vanilla frosting and fresh berries arranged in the design of the American flag. Molly's family would have had to save their butter and sugar rations to make this festive cake, but it would have been perfect for a summertime gathering. To make a layer cake, divide the batter between two 9-inch round cake pans and decrease the cooking time by a few minutes, then use the frosting to sandwich the cakes and frost the top and sides.

MAKES 10 TO 12 SERVINGS

CAKE

3 cups all-purpose flour, plus flour for dusting

2 teaspoons baking powder

¾ teaspoon baking soda

¾ teaspoon salt

1 cup (2 sticks) unsalted butter, at room temperature, plus butter for greasing

2 cups granulated sugar

2 large eggs plus 2 large egg yolks

1 tablespoon vanilla extract

2 cups buttermilk

Preheat the oven to 350°F. Grease a 9-by-13-inch baking pan with butter, line the bottom of the pan with parchment paper, then butter the parchment. Dust with flour, then tap out the excess.

In a medium bowl, sift together the flour, baking powder, baking soda and salt. Set aside. In a large bowl, using an electric mixer, beat the butter and granulated sugar on medium speed until light and fluffy, about 2 minutes. Add the eggs and egg yolks one at a time, beating well after each addition. Beat in the vanilla. Turn off the mixer and scrape down the bowl with a rubber spatula. With the mixer on low speed, beat in the flour mixture in three additions, alternating with the buttermilk in two additions, beginning and ending with the flour and beating just until blended after each addition. Turn off the mixer and scrape down the bowl. Raise the speed to high and beat for 20 seconds. Pour the batter into the prepared pan.

Bake until a wooden skewer inserted into the center of the cake comes out clean, about 55 minutes. Remove the pan from the oven and set it on a wire rack. Let cool for 10 minutes, then run a table knife around the inside edge of the pan. Turn the pan over onto the rack. Lift off the pan and peel off the parchment. Let cool completely.

～ *Continued on page 118* ～

~ *Continued from page 117* ~

VANILLA FROSTING

1 cup (2 sticks) unsalted butter, at room temperature

5 cups powdered sugar

6 tablespoons whole milk

2 teaspoons vanilla extract

¼ teaspoon salt

1 cup blueberries

4 cups raspberries

To make the frosting, in a large bowl, using an electric mixer, beat the butter on medium speed until light and fluffy, about 2 minutes. Reduce the speed to low, add the powdered sugar, milk, vanilla, and salt, and beat just until combined. Turn off the mixer and scrape down the bowl. Beat on medium-high speed until the frosting is airy and smooth, about 5 minutes.

Spread the frosting evenly over the top and sides of the cake. Using the blueberries and raspberries, create the colors of the American flag, with the blueberries arranged in a square in the top-left corner of the cake and the raspberries arranged in thick horizontal stripes across the top of the cake. Cut the cake into wedges and serve.

⭐ Meet Molly McIntire

Molly is a schemer and dreamer growing up in a world full of wartime changes. On the home front, Molly grows vegetables in her victory garden and tries very hard to like them—even the turnips. Around her neck, she wears a silver heart-shaped locket with a picture inside of her father, who's a doctor overseas. Whenever Molly clicks open the locket, Dr. McIntire is always smiling back at her, giving her the courage to do the right thing. Even if that means eating all her turnips.

In Molly's Kitchen

When Molly opened a cupboard or the refrigerator door, she rarely saw sugar, meat, cheese, or butter. Those items were rationed, or limited, so that they could be sent to soldiers fighting overseas. Cookbooks such as *Coupon Cookery* and *Fightin' Food* helped moms plan balanced meals in spite of war shortages. Ground beef took fewer ration stamps than a roast, and women could stretch a pound by making meat loaf, stuffed peppers, or spaghetti sauce. Fruit-flavored gelatin and cupcakes made with applesauce were a way to enjoy sweet treats without using any sugar or butter rations. Americans on the home front felt it was their patriotic duty to scrimp and save wherever they could.

Working Moms

With so many men fighting overseas, America's women were called on to work in factories and fill government jobs. They also stepped in to pump gas, operate railroads, fight fires, and keep farms running. Many women also volunteered for the Red Cross and other organizations that helped the war effort. Women who spent their days out of the house had less time for meal prep and relied on the convenience of packaged foods, such as breakfast cereals and cake mixes, to make cooking easier.

Victory Gardens

People were encouraged to plant gardens and grow their own food so that canned vegetables could be sent to soldiers overseas. Molly was not a fan of the turnips that grew in her family's victory garden, and she didn't love weeding and watering the vegetables, either. But both were sacrifices she was willing to make. The sooner America won the war, the sooner Dad would be home.

Pineapple Upside-Down Cake

Hugely popular in the 1960s, this classic cake used convenience items like canned pineapple slices and maraschino cherries and made regular appearances at family gatherings and church potlucks. This updated version includes fresh pineapple slices and cherries poached with spices. If fresh cherries aren't in season, use jarred Morello cherries and skip poaching them.

MAKES 6 TO 8 SERVINGS

PINEAPPLE TOPPING

3 cups water

1½ cups granulated sugar

2 cinnamon sticks

6 whole allspice

3 tablespoons crystallized ginger

1 ripe pineapple, peeled, cored, and sliced ½ inch thick

8 fresh cherries, pitted (optional)

4 tablespoons (½ stick) unsalted butter, melted, plus butter for greasing

1 cup firmly packed light brown sugar

To make the pineapple topping, in a large frying pan or wide saucepan, combine the granulated sugar and 3 cups water. Set the pan over medium-high heat and bring to a boil, stirring to dissolve the sugar. Add the cinnamon sticks, allspice, crystallized ginger, and pineapple slices, making sure that the fruit is covered with the syrup. Cover the pan and simmer until the pineapple is tender when pierced with a fork, 15 to 20 minutes, adding the cherries (if using) during the last 5 minutes of cooking. Remove the pan from the heat, drain the fruit, and set aside.

Butter the bottom and sides of a 10-inch round cake pan or heavy ovenproof frying pan. Line the bottom of the pan with a circle of parchment paper cut to fit. Pour the melted butter into the pan and use a fork to spread the brown sugar evenly over it. Top with 7 or 8 slices of the poached pineapple slices. Reserve any remaining pineapple for another use. Put a whole poached cherry (if using) in the center of each pineapple slice.

Preheat the oven to 325°F.

~ Continued on page 122 ~

~ *Continued from page 121* ~

VANILLA CAKE

1¼ cups cake flour

½ teaspoon baking soda

½ teaspoon salt

½ cup (1 stick)
unsalted butter,
at room temperature

¼ cup firmly packed
brown sugar

3 large eggs, separated

1 teaspoon vanilla extract

½ cup buttermilk

¼ cup granulated sugar

To make the cake batter, in a medium bowl, sift together the flour, baking soda, and salt. Set aside.

In a large bowl, using an electric mixer, beat the butter and brown sugar until the mixture is light in color and fluffy, about 5 minutes. Beat in the egg yolks and vanilla. With the mixer on low speed, beat in the flour mixture in three additions, alternating with the buttermilk in two additions, beginning and ending with the flour and beating just until blended after each addition. Turn off the mixer and scrape down the bowl with a rubber spatula.

In a clean bowl, using the electric mixer with clean attachments, beat the egg whites until soft peaks form, 2 to 3 minutes. Slowly pour in the granulated sugar while continuing to beat until the mixture firms up slightly. Using a rubber spatula, fold the egg whites into the batter. Pour the batter over the pineapple, spreading it evenly.

Bake until the cake is golden brown and a wooden skewer inserted into the center comes out clean, 35 to 40 minutes. The top should feel slightly firm to the touch. Remove the pan from the oven and set it on a wire rack. Let cool in the pan for 10 minutes, then place a serving plate on top of the pan and, holding the plate and pan together, invert them. Gently lift off the pan, being careful not to burn yourself. If the parchment is stuck to the cake, carefully peel it off. Serve warm.

Fresh Peach Pie

There's no better summer dessert than a fresh peach pie. Juicy, ripe peaches encased in a flaky golden crust conjure warm evenings, lingering over farm-to-table dinners outside, and summer vacations at B&Bs like the one Blaire's family ran.

MAKES 6 TO 8 SERVINGS

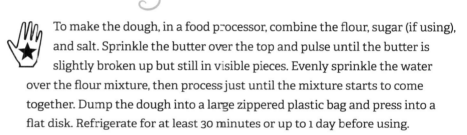

PIE DOUGH FOR DOUBLE CRUST

2 cups all-purpose flour, plus flour for dusting

1 tablespoon sugar (optional)

½ teaspoon salt

¾ cup (1½ sticks) cold unsalted butter, cut into small pieces

½ cup very cold water, plus more if needed

PEACH FILLING

¾ cup sugar

3 tablespoons tapioca starch

Pinch of salt

6 or 7 ripe but firm peaches, peeled, pitted, and sliced ½ inch thick

1 tablespoon cold unsalted butter, cut into pieces

To make the dough, in a food processor, combine the flour, sugar (if using), and salt. Sprinkle the butter over the top and pulse until the butter is slightly broken up but still in visible pieces. Evenly sprinkle the water over the flour mixture, then process just until the mixture starts to come together. Dump the dough into a large zippered plastic bag and press into a flat disk. Refrigerate for at least 30 minutes or up to 1 day before using.

Position a rack in the lower third of the oven and preheat to 375°F. Sprinkle a work surface with flour. Dump the dough onto the floured surface and cut it in half. Roll each half into a 12-inch round about ⅛ inch thick. Transfer 1 dough round to a 9-inch pie dish. Using kitchen scissors or a knife, trim the dough edges, leaving a ¾-inch overhang. Fold the overhang under itself around the rim of the dish, then use a fork to crimp the edge. Cover with plastic wrap and freeze for 30 minutes. Set the second dough round in a cool place until ready to use.

To make the filling, in a small bowl, stir together the sugar, tapioca, and salt. Place the peaches in a large bowl, sprinkle with the sugar mixture, and toss to distribute evenly. Transfer the peaches to the dough-lined pan. Dot with the butter. Position the reserved dough round over the filling. Using kitchen scissors or a knife, trim the edges, leaving a 1-inch overhang. Fold the edge of the top round under the edge of the bottom round and crimp the edges to seal. Using a small knife, cut 5 or 6 slits in the top.

Bake the pie until the crust is golden and the filling is thick and bubbling, about 1 hour. Let cool completely on a wire rack. Cut the pie into wedges and serve.

123

Carrot Cake with Cream Cheese Frosting

One of the most popular desserts of the 1970s, carrot cake was considered a "healthy" alternative to other treats. This sheet cake version is perfect for a potluck or for celebrating a win with a team of hungry athletes, like Julie's basketball team. For a layer cake, divide the batter between two 9-inch round pans, and decrease the baking time by about 10 minutes.

MAKES 10 TO 12 SERVINGS

CARROT CAKE

Unsalted butter, for greasing

2 cups cake flour, plus flour for dusting

2 teaspoons baking powder

2 teaspoons baking soda

1 teaspoon salt

1 teaspoon ground cinnamon

¼ teaspoon ground nutmeg

1½ cups granulated sugar

4 large eggs

1¼ cups canola oil

Finely grated zest of 1 orange

1 pound carrots, peeled and finely grated (about 3 cups)

CREAM CHEESE FROSTING

1 (8-ounce) package cream cheese, at room temperature

4 tablespoons (½ stick) unsalted butter, at room temperature

2 teaspoons vanilla extract

1 cup powdered sugar, sifted

 Preheat the oven to 350°F. Grease a 9-by-13-inch baking pan with butter. Dust the pan with flour, then tap out any excess.

To make the cake, sift together the flour, baking powder, baking soda, salt, cinnamon, and nutmeg onto a sheet of parchment paper. Set aside.

In a large bowl, whisk together the granulated sugar, eggs, oil, and orange zest until thoroughly combined. Stir in the carrots. Using a rubber spatula, fold in the flour mixture just until incorporated. Pour the batter into the prepared pan.

Bake until a wooden skewer inserted into the center of the cake comes out clean, 35 to 40 minutes. Watch closely at the end so that the cake does not overbake. Remove the pan from the oven and set it on a wire rack. Let cool for 15 minutes. Invert the cake onto the rack and let cool completely. Cover with a clean, slightly damp kitchen towel so that the outside does not dry out.

To make the frosting, in a large bowl, using an electric mixer, beat the cream cheese, butter, and vanilla on medium-high speed until light and fluffy, about 2 minutes. Gradually beat in the powdered sugar and beat until thoroughly combined. If the consistency is too soft, refrigerate the frosting until it is spreadable, about 15 minutes.

Transfer the cooled cake to a platter. Using an icing spatula, frost the top and sides of the cake with a thick layer of cream cheese frosting and serve.

★ Meet Julie Albright

Moving to an apartment in San Francisco after her parents' divorce, Julie feels uncertain about the changes in her life. Then a new neighbor brings homemade zucchini bread to welcome Julie, her mom, and her sister to the neighborhood. As they unpack, Mom orders Chinese takeout for dinner, and life starts to look up. On the weekend, Julie and Dad ride the cable car to the Ghirardelli Chocolate Company to watch chocolate being made!

In Julie's Kitchen

After school, Julie helps Mom in her store—and helps get dinner ready, too. As more women began working outside the home in the 1970s, like Julie's mom, restaurant takeout became popular, and new kitchen appliances made meal prep easier.

- Microwave ovens popularized heat-and-eat meals and convenience foods.
- Food processors saved time by chopping, slicing, and blending ingredients quickly.
- Slow cookers gently cooked a one-dish meal all day, so busy moms like Julie's could prep dinner before work. In the evening, Julie's family would come home to a fully cooked meal!

Popular Recipes in Julie's Time

Carrot cake: Health foods were big in the 1970s. Carrot cake was seen as "healthy" because it was made with carrots.

Casseroles: This baked dish has a protein, vegetables, and something starchy (like potatoes). It's easy to throw together on a weeknight, so single-parent families like Julie's could make it quickly.

Watergate salad: This "salad" called for pistachio-flavored Jell-O, pineapple, whipped cream, marshmallows, and chopped nuts. Rumor has it that it was named after the infamous Watergate scandal of President Nixon's presidency.

New Foods!

With factories churning out new products faster than ever, Julie's generation saw a flood of popular new snacks and dinners that we still see in grocery stores today!

- Hamburger Helper (1971)
- Pop Rocks (1975)
- Ben & Jerry's (1978)
- Cup O' Noodles (1978)
- Hubba Bubba Bubble Gum (1979)

Chocolate-Caramel Bundt "Election" Cake

The first presidential election took place in 1788, electing George Washington—who, like Felicity, hailed from Virginia—as the first president of the United States. Election Day became an important holiday to celebrate with special treats, like this over-the-top chocolate Bundt cake drizzled with plenty of caramel sauce. For a modern twist, sprinkle flaky sea salt on top with a scoop of vanilla ice cream or whipped cream (page 130).

MAKES 10 TO 12 SERVINGS

4 tablespoons (½ stick) unsalted butter, plus butter for greasing

3 ounces bittersweet chocolate, coarsely chopped

1 cup all-purpose flour, plus flour for dusting

1 cup sugar

½ cup unsweetened natural cocoa powder

1½ teaspoons baking soda

¼ teaspoon salt

2 large eggs

1 cup buttermilk

2 teaspoons vanilla extract

2¼ cups store-bought caramel sauce

Flaky sea salt (optional)

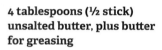

Preheat the oven to 350°F. Grease a 10-cup Bundt pan with butter, making sure to coat all the crevices. Dust the pan with flour, then tap out any excess.

In a saucepan, combine the butter and chocolate. Set the pan over low heat and slowly melt the butter and chocolate, stirring to combine. Remove the pan from the heat and set aside. In a large bowl, whisk together the flour, sugar, cocoa powder, baking soda, and salt. Using an electric mixer, beat in the following ingredients one at a time on low speed, mixing just until combined after each addition: the chocolate mixture, eggs, buttermilk, and vanilla. Raise the speed to high and beat until light and fluffy, about 3 minutes. Pour the batter into the prepared pan, spreading it evenly.

Bake until a wooden skewer inserted near the center of the cake comes out clean, 40 to 45 minutes. Remove the pan from the oven and set it on a wire rack. Let cool for about 15 minutes. Invert the cake onto the rack, lift off the pan, and let cool completely. (The cake can be baked and cooled up to 8 hours in advance. Loosely cover it and keep at room temperature.)

Set the rack with the cake on it on a rimmed baking sheet to catch any drips. Pour the caramel sauce over the top of the cake, allowing it to flow down the sides. Sprinkle with flaky sea salt (if using). Carefully transfer the cake to a cake plate, cut into wedges, and serve.

Strawberry Icebox Pie

No-bake (or little bake) desserts were popular in the 1960s. Cool and creamy, this pie would be a great addition to the 4th of July barbecue Melody's family hosted every year. The pie only needs minutes in the oven to set and the filling is bursting with fresh strawberry flavor. For a special presentation, top the pie with fresh strawberries.

MAKES 6 TO 8 SERVINGS

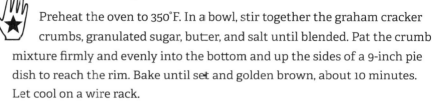

CRUST

1½ cups graham cracker crumbs (12 whole crackers)

¼ cup granulated sugar

6 tablespoons (¾ stick) unsalted butter, melted and cooled

⅛ teaspoon salt

STRAWBERRY FILLING

1 tablespoon (1 package) powdered unflavored gelatin

3 cups hulled and chopped fresh strawberries (about 1¼ pounds berries)

1 tablespoon fresh lemon juice

4 ounces cream cheese, at room temperature

2 teaspoons vanilla extract

¾ cup powdered sugar

1½ cups heavy cream

Preheat the oven to 350°F. In a bowl, stir together the graham cracker crumbs, granulated sugar, butter, and salt until blended. Pat the crumb mixture firmly and evenly into the bottom and up the sides of a 9-inch pie dish to reach the rim. Bake until set and golden brown, about 10 minutes. Let cool on a wire rack.

To make the filling, in a microwave-safe bowl, whisk together the gelatin and 3 tablespoons water. Set aside. In a food processor, combine the strawberries and lemon juice and purée until smooth. Pour the purée into a fine-mesh sieve set over a bowl. Use a rubber spatula to press the purée through the sieve, then discard the seeds. In a bowl, using an electric mixer, beat together the cream cheese and vanilla on medium-low speed until blended. Turn off the mixer, sift the powdered sugar over the cream cheese, and pour in the cream. Beat on low just until the mixture thickens, about 1 minute. Do not overbeat.

Add ¼ cup of the strawberry purée to the gelatin mixture. Microwave on high just until hot, about 30 seconds, then whisk until the gelatin dissolves. Pour the gelatin mixture into the bowl with the remaining strawberry purée and stir to combine. Pour the strawberry mixture into the cream cheese mixture. Using the spatula, gently fold the two mixtures together until evenly blended.

Pour the filling into the cooled crust and smooth the top with the spatula. Cover and refrigerate until set, about 2 hours. Cut into wedges and serve.

Vanilla Chiffon Cake with Tropical Fruit

Nanea and her family enjoyed the delicious tropical fruits of Hawaii—like passion fruit, guava, pineapple, papaya, coconut, and mango—often used to flavor shave ice and other sweet treats. This ultralight vanilla chiffon cake features those luscious fruits and whipped cream. Arrange the filling just short of the edge of the cake layer to keep any fruit or cream from escaping.

MAKES 8 SERVINGS

VANILLA CHIFFON CAKE

1 cup cake flour

1 teaspoon baking powder

½ cup sugar

¼ cup canola oil

1 teaspoon vanilla extract

2 large eggs, separated

¼ teaspoon salt

⅛ teaspoon cream of tartar

Preheat the oven to 350°F. Line a 9-by-2-inch round cake pan with parchment paper (do not butter the pan or parchment).

To make the cake, in a small bowl, sift together the flour and baking powder. Whisk in ¼ cup of the sugar. In a large bowl, whisk together the oil, vanilla, egg yolks, and ¼ cup water. Set aside.

In a medium bowl, using an electric mixer, beat the egg whites, salt, and cream of tartar on medium speed until the egg whites are frothy, about 3 minutes. Slowly add the remaining ¼ cup sugar and beat just until stiff peaks form, about 5 minutes. Whisk the flour mixture into the oil mixture, then fold, then fold in the egg whites. Scrape the batter into the prepared pan.

Bake until a wooden skewer inserted into the center of the cake comes out clean, about 15 minutes. Remove the pan from the oven and set it on a wire rack. Let cool for about 15 minutes. Run a table knife around the inside edge of the pan, then invert the cake onto the rack, lift off the pan, and peel off the parchment. Let cool completely.

~ Continued on page 130 ~

~ *Continued from page 129* ~

TROPICAL FRUIT

1 pound mixed tropical fruits, such as mango, pineapple, and papaya, cut into small chunks

1 teaspoon finely grated lemon zest

¼ cup sugar

2 passion fruits

WHIPPED CREAM

1 cup heavy cream

1 tablespoon sugar

1 teaspoon vanilla extract

While the cake cools, prepare the fruit: In a large bowl, stir together the mixed fruit, sugar, and lemon zest. Halve the passion fruits crosswise, then scoop out the insides into the bowl. Stir until combined.

To make the whipped cream, in a bowl, using the electric mixer, beat together the cream, sugar, and vanilla. Beat on medium-high speed until medium peaks form, about 3 minutes.

Using a long serrated knife, split the cake in half horizontally. Carefully place the bottom half, cut side up, on a platter. Top with half of the fruit mixture, including some of the juices, spreading it into an even layer. Top the fruit with half of the whipped cream, leaving a 1-inch border around the edge. Place the top half of the cake, cut side down, on top of the whipped cream and top with the remaining whipped cream. Spoon the remaining fruit on top. Slice the cake into wedges and serve.

Day at the Beach Cupcakes

When the surf's up, Joss and her best friend head to the beach. These cute
vanilla cupcakes are the perfect way to celebrate a sunny day, whether
you can wiggle your toes in the sand or not. A swirl of fluffy blue frosting looks
like ocean waves, and vanilla cookie crumbs become a delicious sandy beach.
The finishing touch? A colorful paper "beach" umbrella!

MAKES 12 CUPCAKES

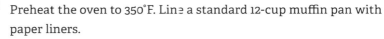

1¼ cups all-purpose flour

1¼ teaspoons
baking powder

¼ teaspoon salt

6 tablespoons (¾ stick)
unsalted butter, at
room temperature

¾ cup sugar

2 large eggs

1 teaspoon vanilla extract

⅓ cup whole milk

Blue gel food coloring

1 cup plain vanilla cookies,
such as Nilla wafers

1½ cups store-bought
vanilla frosting

12 paper umbrellas

Preheat the oven to 350°F. Line a standard 12-cup muffin pan with paper liners.

In a medium bowl, whisk together the flour, baking powder, and salt. In a large bowl, using an electric mixer, beat the butter and sugar on medium-high speed until light and fluffy, 2 to 3 minutes. Add the eggs one at a time, beating well after each addition. Beat in the vanilla. Turn off the mixer and scrape down the bowl with a rubber spatula. Add about half of the flour mixture and beat on low speed just until blended. Beat in the milk and a few drops of blue food coloring. Add the remaining flour mixture and beat just until blended. Divide the batter evenly among the prepared muffin cups.

Bake until the tops are light golden brown and a wooden skewer inserted into the center of a cupcake comes out clean, 18 to 20 minutes. Remove the pan from the oven and set it on a wire rack. Let cool for 10 minutes, then carefully transfer the cupcakes directly to the rack. Let cool completely.

Meanwhile, place the cookies in a zippered plastic bag. Using a rolling pin, roll over the cookies until finely ground. Transfer the crumbs to a plate. Using a small spatula, cover half of each cupcake with some frosting, then dip the frosted portion into the cookie crumbs. Add 5 or 6 drops of blue food coloring to the remaining frosting in the bowl and stir to combine. Top the remaining half of each cupcake with the blue frosting. Place a paper umbrella into the "sand" on each cupcake and serve.

Apple Bread Pudding

Bread pudding is a good use of ingredients that would otherwise be wasted—something resourceful Kit would appove of. Soaking stale bread in an eggy custard transforms. Studded with chewy dried apples and currants and flavored with warm spices, this bread pudding is the ideal comfort food on a cold night.

MAKES 6 SERVINGS

**Unsalted butter,
for greasing**

**4 thick slices day-old
challah or soft eggy bread,
cut into ½-inch cubes**

**1 cup dried apples,
roughly chopped**

**2 tablespoons dried
currants or raisins**

1½ cups half-and-half

2 large eggs

**¼ cup firmly packed
light brown sugar**

1 teaspoon vanilla extract

**2 teaspoons
ground cinnamon**

**⅛ teaspoon
ground nutmeg**

**1 tablespoon
granulated sugar**

**Whipped Cream, for
serving (page 130)**

Preheat the oven to 325°F. Butter a 9-by-13-inch baking dish. Scatter the bread cubes evenly in the prepared dish. Top evenly with the apples and currants.

In a large bowl, whisk together the half-and-half, eggs, brown sugar, vanilla, 1 teaspoon of the cinnamon, and the nutmeg until smooth. Slowly pour the custard mixture over the bread and fruits. Let stand at room temperature for about 30 minutes so that the bread soaks up the custard mixture, occasionally pressing down on the bread cubes and fruit with a spatula to keep the bread moist.

In a small bowl, stir together the remaining 1 teaspoon cinnamon and the granulated sugar and sprinkle the mixture evenly over the pudding.

Bake until the top is golden brown and the bread cubes on the top are crisp, about 1 hour. Remove the baking dish from the oven and set it on a wire rack. Let cool for about 20 minutes. Serve warm with whipped cream.

New York Cherry Cheesecake

This specific style of cheesecake was invented in Rebecca's home town of New York. Be careful not to overbake the cake or it will crack as it cools. For a lemony version, add 2 teaspoons grated lemon zest to the filling along with the vanilla. Instead of the cherry topping, serve wedges of cheesecake with sliced fresh strawberries or peaches.

Makes 8 to 10 servings

CRUST

1 cup graham cracker crumbs (8 whole crackers)

½ cup slivered almonds

3 tablespoons sugar

4 tablespoons (¼ stick) unsalted butter, melted, plus butter for greasing

FILLING

4 (8-ounce) packages cream cheese, at room temperature

2 tablespoons all-purpose flour

¼ teaspoon salt

1¼ cups sugar

½ cup sour cream

1 tablespoon vanilla extract

3 large eggs

 Preheat the oven to 350°F. Grease a 9-inch springform pan with butter.

In a food processor, combine the graham cracker crumbs, almonds, and sugar and process until finely ground. Drizzle in the melted butter and pulse until evenly moistened. Pat the crumb mixture firmly and evenly into the bottom and 1½ inches up the sides of the prepared pan. Bake until golden, about 7 minutes. Remove the pan from the oven and set it on a wire rack. Let cool completely. Reduce the oven temperature to 300°F.

To make the filling, in a large bowl, using an electric mixer, beat the cream cheese, flour, and salt on medium-high speed until smooth. Add the sugar, sour cream, and vanilla and beat until blended. Add the eggs one at a time, beating well after each addition. Pour the filling into the cooled crust.

Bake until the filling is set but the center still jiggles slightly when the pan is gently shaken, about 1 hour. (The filling will firm as it cools.) Remove the pan from the oven and set it on a wire rack. Run a table knife around the inside edge of the pan to loosen the cheesecake. Let cool to room temperature. Cover and refrigerate until chilled, at least 3 hours.

~ Continued on page 136 ~

~ *Continued from page 135* ~

CHERRY TOPPING

1 pound fresh cherries, pitted and halved

½ cup cherry juice

¼ cup sugar

Salt

1 tablespoon cornstarch

To make the topping, in a saucepan, combine the cherries, cherry juice, sugar, and a pinch of salt. Set the pan over medium-high heat and cook, stirring, until the cherries soften, 2 to 3 minutes. In a bowl, stir together the cornstarch and 1 tablespoon water, then add to the cherry mixture. Cook just until the liquid comes to a boil and thickens, about 3 minutes.

Remove from the heat and and carefully transfer the cherry mixture to a bowl to cool. Remove the pan sides. Place the cheesecake on a plate and top with the cherry mixture. Cut the cheesecake into wedges and serve.

Chocolate, Vanilla & Raspberry Swirl Cake

Bright, bold patterns were Courtney's style and this cake, with its epic swirls of chocolate, vanilla, and raspberry, certainly fits the bill. It's also the perfect addition to a fun sleepover or video-game night.

MAKES 8 TO 10 SERVINGS

2¼ cups all-purpose flour, plus flour for dusting

1 tablespoon baking powder

¼ teaspoon salt

½ cup (1 stick) plus 2 tablespoons unsalted butter, at room temperature, plus butter for greasing

1¾ cups sugar

1 teaspoon vanilla extract

3 large eggs, at room temperature

1¼ cups whole milk, at room temperature

2 tablespoons unsweetened cocoa powder

2 tablespoons very hot water

⅛ teaspoon raspberry extract

Red gel food coloring

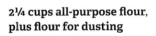 Preheat the oven to 350°F. Grease a 9-inch springform pan with 2-inch sides with butter. Line the pan bottom with parchment paper, cut to fit exactly. Grease the paper with butter. Dust the pan with flour, then tap out any excess.

For the vanilla batter, in a medium bowl, stir together the flour, baking powder, and salt. Set aside. In a large bowl, using an electric mixer, beat the butter, sugar, and vanilla on medium speed until creamy, about 3 minutes. Add the eggs one at a time, beating well after each addition. With the mixer on low speed, beat in the flour mixture in three additions, alternating with the milk in two additions, beginning and ending with the flour mixture and beating just until blended after each addition.

For the chocolate batter, in a small bowl, stir together the cocoa powder and hot water until smooth. Add 1 cup of the vanilla batter and stir until blended. For the raspberry batter, in a small bowl, stir together ½ cup of the vanilla batter, the raspberry extract, and a few drops of red food coloring until blended.

Pour the remaining vanilla batter into the prepared pan, spreading it evenly. Add the chocolate batter in big globs over the vanilla, then drizzle the raspberry batter over the top. Draw the tip of a table knife through the batter, making several swirls and gently pushing all the way through to the bottom of the pan.

Bake until golden and a wooden skewer inserted into the center of the cake comes out clean, 45 to 50 minutes. Let cool for 10 minutes on a wire rack. Remove the pan sides, invert the cake onto a rack, remove the pan bottom, peel off the parchment, and invert again onto the rack. Let cool completely. Cut the cake into wedges and serve.

Addy

⭐

Sweet Potato Pie

Sweet potatoes were bountiful in the South and easier to grow than pumpkins, so a tradition of making sweet potato pies grew from Southern plantations. Addy and her brother, Sam, loved their mother's sweet potato pie. For the best results, be sure to bake this pie gently, just until the filling is set but still has a slight wobble. Serve it with a big dollop of lightly whipped cream.

MAKES 6 TO 8 SERVINGS

PIE DOUGH

1¼ cups all-purpose flour, plus flour for dusting

1 tablespoon granulated sugar (optional)

¼ teaspoon salt

½ cup (1 stick) cold unsalted butter, cut into small pieces

3 tablespoons very cold water, plus more if needed

1 large egg beaten with 1 teaspoon water

To make the dough, in a food processor, ccombine the flour, granulated sugar (if using), and salt. Sprinkle the butter over the top and pulse until the butter is slightly broken up but still in visible pieces. Evenly sprinkle the water over the flour mixture, then process just until the mixture starts to come together. Dump the dough into a large zippered plastic bag and press into a flat disk. Refrigerate for at least 30 minutes or up to 1 day before using, or freeze for up to 1 month.

Sprinkle a work surface with flour. Dump the dough onto the floured surface. Roll out the dough into a 12-inch round about ⅛ inch thick. Transfer the dough round to a 9-inch pie dish. Using kitchen scissors or a knife, trim the dough edges, leaving a ¾-inch overhang. Fold the overhand under itself around the rim of the dish, brush with the egg mixture, and use a fork to crimp the edges. Cover with plastic wrap and freeze for 30 minutes.

Meanwhile, preheat the oven to 350°F. Line the pie shell with aluminum foil and fill with pie weights, dried beans, or uncooked rice. Bake until the pie shell is lightly browned, about 20 minutes. Remove the pie dish from the oven and carefully remove the foil and weights. Set the dish on a wire rack and let cool completely. Keep the oven set.

~ *Continued on page 140* ~

~ *Continued from page 139* ~

FILLING

2 cups peeled, cooked, and mashed sweet potatoes (from about 2½ pounds sweet potatoes)

1 cup firmly packed light brown sugar

4 tablespoons (½ stick) unsalted butter, melted and cooled

1 teaspoon ground cinnamon

½ teaspoon salt

¼ teaspoon ground nutmeg

1 (12-ounce) can evaporated milk

3 large eggs

1 tablespoon vanilla extract

Whipped Cream, for serving (page 130)

Pecans for decorating

To make the filling, in a food processor, blend the sweet potatoes until smooth. Add the brown sugar, melted butter, cinnamon, salt, nutmeg, evaporated milk, eggs, and vanilla and process until smooth, stopping the processor occasionally to scrape down the sides with a spatula. Pour the filling into the cooled crust.

Bake until the center is just set and the filling is golden brown, 45 to 50 minutes. If the edges of the crust are browning too quickly, cover them loosely with wide strips of aluminum foil. Remove the pie dish from the oven and set it on a wire rack. Let cool completely. Cut the pie into wedges and serve with dollops of whipped cream and pecans.

⭐ Meet Addy Walker

Addy and her mother make the courageous decision to escape the plantation where they live as slaves in 1864. Addy's Poppa and brother, Sam, have already been sold away by Master Stevens, and the family's plan is to reunite in the city of Philadelphia. Addy's journey to freedom is long and dangerous. When she and Momma arrive at the docks in Philadelphia, they are met by members of the AME Baptist church. At the church, Addy savors her first meal in freedom and wonders what her new life will bring.

Foods from the South

In Philadelphia, Addy and Momma prepared many of the same foods they had eaten on the plantation. There, every slave received a certain amount of cornmeal each week, which was mixed with water to make breads, cakes, and dumplings.

Plantation owners sometimes allowed enslaved people to have small vegetable gardens. The water the vegetables had been cooked in was called pot likker. Families dunked corn bread into the pot likker so nothing would go to waste.

Momma made sweet potato pudding for Christmas in Philadelphia, just as she had on the plantation, and Addy looked forward to hoppin' John—a mixture of black-eyed peas, rice, and bacon—for their New Year's Day good-luck tradition.

New Foods in the North

When Addy started living in Philadelphia, she began to eat foods that she and her family didn't have on the plantation. At church socials, she had creamy potato salad, lemonade, and wonderful desserts like juicy peach cobbler.

Poppa fixed up a broken old ice cream freezer he found in the street, and Addy loved to take a turn at the crank. Soon there was a taste of sweet homemade ice cream for everyone.

Addy especially loved to help stir a big bowl of pound cake batter at the boarding house where she lived with her family. Pound cake got its name from the ingredients that went into it in Addy's time—a pound of flour, a pound of sugar, a pound eggs, and a pound of butter!

Fruit & Cream Pavlova

Pavlova, named after Russian ballerina Anna Pavlova, is a luscious dessert of crisp-chewy meringue topped with pillowy whipped cream and plenty of tart-sweet fruit. It was invented in Australia or New Zealand and is a popular dessert Down Under, especially for celebrations and holidays. Kiwifruit and strawberries are traditional toppings, but add whatever ripe fruits you love, like slices of fresh mango or peaches, a mixture of berries, or pitted fresh cherries.

MAKES 6 TO 8 SERVINGS

4 large egg whites

1 tablespoon cornstarch

**1 cup plus
1 tablespoon sugar**

2 teaspoons vanilla extract

1 teaspoon lemon juice

1½ cups heavy cream

**2 cups mixed berries,
such as blueberries,
blackberries, and sliced
strawberries**

**2 kiwifruit, peeled and
peeled and sliced crosswise**

Position a rack in the lower third of the oven and preheat the oven to 300°F. Using an 11-inch round plate as a guide, trace a circle around the plate on a sheet of parchment paper. Turn the parchment paper over and place on a cookie sheet.

In a large bowl, using an electric mixer, beat the egg whites on medium speed until well mixed. Sprinkle the cornstarch over the egg whites and beat until the whites are foamy, about 1 minute. Raise the speed to high and very gradually add the 1 cup sugar, beating until stiff, shiny peaks form when the beaters are lifted (turn off the mixer first!), about 6 minutes. Beat in 1 teaspoon of the vanilla and the lemon juice. Using a large spoon, spread the meringue into the circle drawn on the parchment. Make a depression in the center of the meringue so the outside edges are higher, creating a bowl-like surface.

Bake until the meringue is crispy and looks dry, about 45 minutes. Turn off the oven, crack open the door, and let the meringue cool in the oven for 1 hour. Transfer the meringue to a serving plate and remove the parchment paper.

In a medium bowl, using an electric mixer, beat the cream and the remaining 1 tablespoon sugar and 1 teaspoon vanilla on medium-high speed until soft peaks form. Spoon the whipped cream into the center of the meringue. Top with the berries and kiwifruit. Cut the pavlova into slices and serve.

143

weldon**owen**

PO Box 3088
San Rafael, CA 94912
www.weldonowen.com

WELDON OWEN INTERNATIONAL
CEO Raoul Goff
Publisher Roger Shaw
Associate Publisher Amy Marr
Editorial Assistant Jourdan Plautz
VP of Creative Chrissy Kwasnik
Senior Designer Judy Wiatrek Trum

Managing Editor Katie Killebrew
Production Manager Sam Taylor
VP of Manufacturing Alix Nicholaeff

Photographer Nicole Hill Gerulat
Food Stylist Carrie Purcell
Prop Stylist Veronica Olson

AMERICAN GIRL *SWEET & SAVORY TREATS COOKBOOK*
Conceived and produced by Weldon Owen International

Printed and bound in Turkey
10 9 8 7 6 5 4 3 2 1

Library of Congress Cataloging in Publication
data is available

ISBN: 13: 978-1-68188-775-3

ACKNOWLEDGMENTS
Weldon Owen wishes to thank the following people for their generous support to help produce this book:
Kris Balloun, Lesley Bruynesteyn, Kim Laidlaw, and Rachel Markowitz.